◆◆◆◆◆◆◆◆◆◆◆◆◆◆◆
Preaching to Latinos
◆◆◆◆◆◆◆◆◆◆◆◆◆◆◆

PREACHING TO LATINOS

WELCOMING THE HISPANIC MOMENT IN THE U.S. CHURCH

◆◆◆◆◆◆◆◆◆◆◆◆◆◆◆◆◆

Michael I. Kueber

Foreword by Hosffman Ospino

The Catholic University of America Press
Washington, D.C.

Copyright © 2023
The Catholic University of America Press

All rights reserved

The paper used in this publication meets the requirements
of American National Standards for Information Science—
Permanence of Paper for Printed Library materials, ANSI Z39.48–1992.

∞

Cataloging-in-Publication data available
from the Library of Congress.

ISBN: 978-0-8132-3624-7 | eISBN: 978-0-8132-3625-4

Book design by Burt&Burt
Text set in Minion Pro, Aleo, and Meta Pro Sans

Contents

Foreword by Hosffman Ospino — VII
Preface — XI

Introduction: The Challenge and the Task — 1
1. Cross-Cultural Preaching: One Example from History — 5
2. The Hispanic Moment — 11
3. The Hispanic Moment and a Theology of Communion — 21
4. Worldviews and U.S. Latinos — 29
5. Sacramentality and Hispanic Popular Religion — 37
6. The Historical Roots of Hispanic Popular Religion — 47
7. Sacramentality and Preaching to Latinos — 57
8. Hispanic Sacramentality and the Sacraments in Youth — 69
9. Hispanic Sacramentality and the Sacraments in Adulthood — 83
10. Hispanic Sacramentality in the Span of the Liturgical Year — 93
11. The Hispanic Moment and Where to Go from Here — 101
    Conclusion — 107

Appendix: Sample Sermons in English and Spanish — 109
Bibliography — 121
Index — 129

Foreword

By Hosffman Ospino

In November 2013, Pope Francis gifted the Catholic world with his apostolic exhortation *The Joy of the Gospel*. There he laid down the building blocks for the evangelizing commitments he wanted his pontificate to inspire. When I learned about the document, I truly hoped that he would say something about preaching. The pope did not disappoint! Anyone entrusted with the ministry of preaching should read the exhortation, particularly chapter 3. I want to lift up the following observation:

> Christian preaching thus finds in the heart of people and their culture a source of living water, which helps the preacher to know what must be said and how to say it. Just as all of us like to be spoken to in our mother tongue, so too in the faith we like to be spoken to in our "mother culture," our native language (cf. 2 Macc 7:21, 27), and our heart is better disposed to listen. This language is a kind of music which inspires encouragement, strength and enthusiasm.[1]

An ecclesial document on the proclamation of the Gospel in our day had to say something about preaching. For most Catholics who attend Mass or other sacramental celebrations, the preaching that takes place within the context of the liturgy is their main source of spiritual and theological reflection in a given week. Because the majority of Catholics in the United States are not regular churchgoers, when they participate in a liturgical celebration that involves preaching, they should receive the very best. There are certainly other opportunities outside the liturgy when preaching happens, and people

---

[1] Francis, *Evangelii Gaudium* [*The Joy of the Gospel*], Apostolic Exhortation, November 24, 2013, accessed June 26, 2017, http://w2.vatican.va/content/francesco/en/apost_exhortations/documents/papa-francesco_esortazione-ap_20131124_evangelii-gaudium.html, n. 139.

there should also hear the Word of God broken open in ways that seek to connect with their lives and transform them.

Preaching is hardly a unidirectional dynamic in which the preacher shares certain ideas—prepared or spontaneous—with the faithful, telling them how to interpret God's Word or suggesting what to do while they receive the message passively. Unfortunately, this is how many preachers in our church often see themselves in relationship to their communities. Preaching should not be treated as an isolated or individualistic exercise. As the previously quoted passage from *The Joy of the Gospel* suggests, preaching is profoundly dialogical and communal.

Preaching begins long before putting one's message into words. It begins with an intentional immersion into *la realidad* (the reality) of the people the preacher has been called to accompany: "The preacher also needs to keep his ear to the people and to discover what it is that the faithful need to hear."[2] Such immersion requires learning about people's questions, concerns, joys, anxieties, fears, and hopes. It demands that the preacher understand the cultural nuances that shape people's lives, including symbols, rituals, and language. Immersion into *la realidad* of the people is an exercise of humble search for the presence of God in the everyday while remaining open to being surprised by God's Holy Spirit. La *realidad diaria* (everyday reality) is "a source of living water," as Pope Francis suggests, from which the preacher drinks to make sure that the message bridges faith and life in creative ways. Before saying something, the preacher must listen attentively to God in prayer, the church's tradition through study, and God's people through accompaniment.

In this book, Fr. Michael Kueber shares his experience as a preacher who for more than two decades has been deeply immersed in faith communities serving Hispanic Catholics: keeping an ear to Latinos and drinking from their wells. About 43 percent of all Catholics in the United States self-identify as Hispanic, as do nearly 60 percent of Catholics younger than eighteen. Most priests serving and preaching in Catholic communities where Latinos worship are white Euro-Americans, like Fr. Michael. These priests, alongside many other pastoral leaders, Hispanic and non-Hispanic, preach week after week in a church that is de facto bilingual (English and Spanish) and increasingly diverse in terms of cultures, languages, races, and ethnicities.

Preaching in Hispanic communities is not an easy task. As the stories and practical examples in this book show, Fr. Michael's experience is deeply grounded in his commitment to accompany immigrants, mainly from Mexico, and their U.S.-born children as they all negotiate religious and social

---

2 Francis, *Evangelii Gaudium*, n. 154.

identities in this country. He reminds us that immigrants make up only a portion of the Hispanic community. In fact, we need to keep in mind that about 64 percent of all Latinos are born in the United States. Preaching in Hispanic faith communities is often done in English, Spanish, and even Spanglish. While the Mexican background of the majority of Latinos in the country calls for particular cultural and religious connections at the time of preaching, those engaged in this ministry also need to learn and develop particular intercultural competencies to serve Latinos whose background is Caribbean, Central American, South American, indigenous, Black, and racially mixed.

As Catholicism in the United States becomes increasingly Hispanic, there is a growing need for preachers and other pastoral agents who understand and embrace the Hispanic Catholic experience with its many nuances. Such an understanding takes time, dedication, intentionality, and, most importantly, love. Besides serving as a preaching manual, this book also provides a general introduction to some of the realities and questions associated with ministry to Hispanic Catholics in parish life. Once again, preaching begins long before putting one's message into words.

Fr. Michael walks his readers through interesting stories about planning *fiestas* and serenades, visiting struggling families, engaging in practices of popular Catholicism, and being in situations when advocacy for justice is urgent. All these realities inspire his preaching. From this book, we get a sense that when he preaches, his words resonate strongly in the hearts and minds of the many Hispanic Catholics who listen to him. When one as a preacher takes the time to sincerely and joyfully walk with one's community, soon one speaks with a language that is, as Pope Francis observes, "a kind of music which inspires encouragement, strength and enthusiasm."[3]

Hosffman Ospino, PhD
Boston College

September 13, 2022
Memorial of Saint John Chrysostom

---

[3] Francis, *Evangelii Gaudium*, n. 139.

Preface

In 2016, I attended a liturgical conference at the University of Notre Dame. One of the keynote speakers was Christian Smith, the well-known sociologist. In his address, "Parents, the *Real* Pastors: On the Centrality of Parenting in Passing on Religious Faith and Practice to the Next Generation," Smith spoke briefly about the catechetical history of the immigrant Catholic Church in the U.S. To begin his presentation, he drew upon his knowledge of sociology and the famous Max Weber who stated that all "isms" have carriers. Lenin was a carrier for Communism as Susan B. Anthony was for feminism. The carriers for Catholicism in the nineteenth-century immigrant church in the U.S. were the immigrant priests, nuns, and parents who established Catholic parishes, parochial schools, and ethnic neighborhoods. All of these served as carriers of Catholicism from one generation to the next. Smith asserts that since the 1960s, all these carriers have disappeared except for parents. Therefore, if the Catholic faith is to be handed on to the next generation, it will happen primarily through the parents.[1]

Smith's research shows that parents are the primary carriers of the Catholic faith. They pass on the faith most effectively to their children when they regularly practice it in the home. Prayer before meals, regular religious instruction, and attending Mass on Sundays all contribute to passing on the faith. Catholic parents must be intentional in this endeavor. Moreover, they can take advantage of teachable moments to teach their children to pray. For example, if they hear a siren, they can take a moment to pray aloud for the safety and protection of those involved. Knowing they are the major carrier of Catholic culture is perhaps frightening for many Catholic parents, but it also should be empowering. Catholic parents can learn the skills they need to pass on the Catholic faith to their children.

Smith did not specifically focus on the problem of passing on the faith to the largest group of Catholic immigrants to fill U.S. churches today: Latinos. That my mind immediately went to them reflects my own experience of

---

[1] Christian Smith and Justin Bartkus, "Parents, the *Real* Pastors: On the Centrality of Parenting in Passing on Religious Faith and Practice to the Next Generation" (lecture, 2016 Liturgy and the New Evangelization Symposium, Notre Dame, Indiana, June 21, 2016).

cross-cultural ministry with Latino parishioners. From the beginning, the origins of this book on preaching to Latinos is grounded in the lived experience of an Anglo priest and catechist trying to evangelize and catechize Latino parents and their teenagers with all the ups and downs involved in such an effort.

My love for the Spanish language began in high school and my friendship with a Mexican student, whose family I visited the summer before my freshman year at the University of Notre Dame. I continued to love the Spanish language and Hispanic culture after graduating from Notre Dame. I served two years in Grenada as a missionary of the People of Praise. During that time, I taught Spanish at the Grenada Boys Secondary School (GBSS). Some of the other Grenadian teachers had studied in Cuba, so I was able to speak Spanish with them regularly. I also was able to visit Venezuela and immerse myself in that culture for a short period of time.

My interest in Spanish and Hispanic culture developed the most, however, with early placements as a transitional deacon and a newly ordained priest. In 1999, the Archbishop of Portland and the seminary placed me in a parish with a large Latino community. I would later serve there for seven years both as parish priest and as a pastor. Two pastoral workers in this parish were especially helpful: Corina and Carlos. Corina was the faith formation director and oversaw weddings and *quinceañeras*. She patiently explained to me in Spanish how to minister in a loving way to Latino Catholics when they approached the parish for faith formation and marriage in the Church. Carlos served as a pastoral assistant. He accompanied me as we visited the sick and dying and as I anointed them with the oil of the sick and prayed the special prayers for the infirmed and those close to death. Like Corina, Carlos was so patient in explaining to me how Latinos viewed sickness, death, and family. During my deacon year, they were my colleagues. Later, they would become pastoral workers serving the Lord and the parish I was called to pastor.

Working full-time for seven years as parish priest and as pastor in a parish with a large community of Latinos was my real education in Hispanic ministry. I daily communicated in Spanish to Carlos, Corina, other staff, and parishioners. I loved preaching regularly in Spanish. I lived the Hispanic spirituality focused on special signs and symbols. I participated in the important sacred moments in the lives of Hispanic parishioners: Baptism, first Communion, Confirmation, marriage, and death. I shared the people's joy as well as their sorrow. These seven years formed me to serve as Jesus served, to be a good shepherd who, as Pope Francis says, took on the smell of the sheep.

In writing this book, I have combined this experience as an Anglo-American priest working with Latinos in ordinary parish life together with the insights of scholars like Christian Smith. Applying Smith's insights on catechesis to cross-cultural preaching has the potential to help pastoral ministers in shared parishes to preach the gospel better to Hispanic parents. Cross-cultural preachers need resources to help them with the task of teaching Hispanic parents how to hand on the Catholic faith to their children. One could call this approach "Catechetical Preaching to Hispanic Parents." Many Hispanic immigrants have a great deal of faith. They practice traditional piety, but they do not know how to explain these practices to their children, some of whom want to know the deeper truths behind them.

Again, Smith's key insight is that all the carriers of faith are gone from these children's lives, except their parents. If the Catholic faith is to be handed on to the next generation of Latinos, it will most likely be through the parents of the current generation. This insight was an *aha moment* for me, and I decided to test this hypothesis. To write my Doctor of Ministry thesis, I decided to prepare Hispanic teenagers for Confirmation with classes which their parents would also attend. I aimed the course at the adults with the hope that they would then pass on the Catholic faith to their children. My results were positive, and I report them in my thesis *Cross-cultural Preaching and Catechesis: Passing on the Faith to the Next Generation*.

My second *aha moment* occurred in the library while reading Justo González and Pablo Jiménez's *Púlpito*. They both describe their experiences preaching to Latinos. I resonated with what they said because it matched my experience of preaching to this demographic as an Anglo-American for the last twenty-three years. These two Protestant theologians understood and, in an ecumenical spirit, I welcomed their insights and scholarship. Nevertheless, I was disheartened because I could not find a similarly practical but insightful work in the Catholic world. And yet the need for such a resource is even greater in the Catholic Church than in the Protestant churches. Because I could not find the book I wanted, I wrote this one.

It began as my doctoral thesis at the Aquinas Institute in St. Louis, Missouri. While the doctoral committee accepted my work and awarded me a doctorate degree in preaching, I began to realize that a thesis does not necessarily appeal to book publishers. Rejection letter after rejection letter made it clear that I needed help navigating the world of trying to publish a book. What was I to do?

Happily, The Lilly Endowment provided money to Aquinas Institute for the purpose of publishing books on preaching. With this financial help, Dr. Rev. Gregory Heille established the Delaplane Preaching Initiative and invited me to be a part of it. In March 2020, before Covid-19 locked down the country, I joined fourteen other scholars in a writing workshop at Our Lady of Guadalupe monastery in Albuquerque, New Mexico. We had already spent about eight months setting goals, offering advice, editing, and holding one another accountable. This writing community and the practice of writing was how I was able to transform a thesis into a book.

In addition to my love for the Spanish language and those who speak it in América, this book brings together several of the great loves of my life: human connection, Scripture, preaching, and the ministerial priesthood. My love for Scripture began and grew in the People of Praise community, which I joined in 1982. I subsequently joined the Brotherhood in 1985. A passion for preaching took root during my diaconate year at Mt. Angel Seminary in Oregon in 1999 and my placement at St. Anne's in Gresham, Oregon. Finally, since my priestly ordination in 2000, a love for the ministerial priesthood is the context in which I have grown and expressed these passions.

I want to thank the people who have helped me along the journey of writing a book, including the cohort at Aquinas and my teachers. Joining the community of writers in the cohort of the Delaplane Preaching Initiative has been invaluable. Dr. Deborah Wilhelm led us with her wisdom, humor, and wit. The last part of this journey has been teaching for two years at The Catholic University in America. I want to thank Very Rev. Mark Morozowich, the Dean for the School of Theology and Religious Studies, who suggested I try to publish my book with The Catholic University of America Press. Dr. Cabrini Pak, a professor of Marketing at the Busch Business School, reviewed the manuscript and offered suggestions and encouragement. John Martino, my acquisitions editor, has given expert advice about editing and how to publish a book. Julie Conroy from the People of Praise reviewed the text and offered corrections and comments. Joanie McMahon provided illustrations and Emily Putzke has assisted with research. Joanie and Emily are members of the Franciscan Mission Service community, of which my niece Grace Kueber also is a member. I want to thank the ten men in my community, The Brotherhood of the People of Praise, for their prayers and support. Finally, I want to thank my dad, Ron Kueber, my mom, Christine Kueber, and my other family members who have been so supportive in this endeavor.

Preaching to Latinos

Introduction

The Challenge and the Task

The demography of the Roman Catholic Church in the United States today is marked by diversity. Waves of immigration from Latin America and Asia have contributed to this transformation. The experience of Catholicism in the United States differs from other areas of the world: "The Roman Catholic Church in the United States is the most ethnically and racially diverse national ecclesial body in the world."[1] Approximate percentages of the different races and ethnicities found in Catholicism in the United States are as follows: 47% Euro-American, White; 43% Hispanic; 5% Asian/Pacific Islander; 4% African American/Black; and 1% Native American. This picture of Catholicism in the United States is quite different from what it was in the 1950s when Euro-American, White Catholics constituted about ninety percent of all Catholics in the country.[2] What are the reasons for this dramatic change in the last sixty years? Hosffman Ospino cites two reasons behind this change: globalization and new migration patterns.[3]

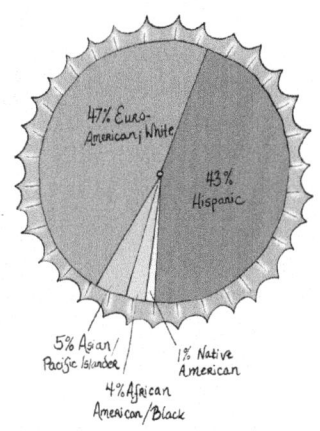

Source: Joanie McMahon.

---

1 Timothy Matovina, *Latino Catholicism: Transformation in America's Largest Church* (Princeton, NJ: Princeton University Press, 2012), 38.

2 Hosffman Ospino, *Interculturalism and Catechesis: A Catechist's Guide to Responding to Cultural Diversity* (New London, CT: Twenty-Third Publications, 2017), 20. See also Zech et al., *Catholic Parishes of the 21st Century* (New York: Oxford University Press, 2017), 11.

3 Ospino, 15.

Rather than form ethnic or national parishes like European Catholic immigrants did in the nineteenth and early twentieth centuries, many of these new Catholic immigrants joined already existing parishes, creating **shared parishes**.[4] "The term 'shared parishes' describes parish communities in which two or more languages or cultural contexts are an integral part of the ministerial life and mission of a particular parish."[5] I have served as a deacon, parochial vicar, and pastor in two shared parishes, one on the West Coast and the other in the Midwest. Both parishes are approximately eighty percent Hispanic[6] and have more Sunday Masses in Spanish than in English. In addition to Sunday Masses, both parishes celebrate a large number of liturgies in Spanish, such as Baptisms, first Communions, *quinceañeras*, Confessions, Confirmations, and weddings.

Among the many challenges of pastoral ministry in shared parishes, one particularly difficult challenge is cross-cultural and intergenerational preaching. In the Hispanic ministry context, preachers have the weekly task of trying to preach the gospel not only to immigrants from the Southern Hemisphere, but also to their children. The challenge preachers encounter every weekend is how to preach both in an intergenerational manner and cross-culturally to the first-generation Latino immigrants, to their second-generation Hispanic immigrant children, and increasingly to third-generation Latinos, and often to do all this cross-culturally. Preaching to these three groups may be compared to archers shooting arrows to hit a bullseye. When cross-cultural preachers preach well to even one of these distinct groups, they hit the bullseye. The challenge of cross-cultural and intergenerational preaching is often preachers do not know whether they have communicated well with the congregation. They do not know where the arrow has landed. How do cross-cultural and intergenerational preachers come to know where the arrow has landed? How do they know when they have successfully reached across a cultural, linguistic, and ethnic divide and communicated well both to Hispanic parents and to their children?

The large presence of immigrants and different ethnicities in parishes presents unique challenges to preachers. The first challenge is the language. Trying to preach in one's own language is a difficult enough task. How much more difficult, then, is it to preach in a different language? The next great challenge is the difference in culture. The immigrant's culture is different

---

4 Brett Hoover, *The Shared Parish: Latinos, Anglos, and the Future of U.S. Catholicism* (New York: New York University Press, 2014), 2–3.

5 United States Conference of Catholic Bishops, *Best Practices for Shared Parishes: So That They May All Be One* (Washington, D.C.: United States Conference of Catholic Bishops, 2014), 1.

6 The adjectives Hispanic and Latino are used interchangeably.

Source: "Youth Praying" by Richard Masoner, CC BY-SA 2.0, via Wikimedia Commons.

from the dominant culture of the United States. The preacher must seek to bridge the gap between (at least) two distinct cultures. If this is not achieved, misunderstanding occurs, and the preacher fails to communicate the gospel effectively.

What is needed to meet this challenge? Preachers should reflect upon the larger picture of what is necessary to improve cross-cultural preaching. In an article on the relationship between preaching and doctrine, Michael Connors and Ann Garrido explain doctrinal and catechetical preaching. They refer to Luke Timothy Johnson's five essential contributions of the Christian creeds, in which Johnson states that "the creed 'constructs a world,' i.e., it provides a kind of imaginative hermeneutical key through which all reality is refracted. This is a key that both opens up an understanding of reality and existence while standing in contrast to other systems of belief."[7] A "creed" for cross-cultural preaching to Latinos in the U.S. is needed today. This "creed" is a Hispanic hermeneutic and involves inculturation. A hermeneutic is a way of approaching the Scriptures, Tradition, and theology that leads to effective preaching, teaching, and pastoral care. With the help of a Hispanic hermeneutic, the Anglo preacher finds resources to become thoroughly one with his Hispanic audience. The cross-cultural preacher

---

7 Michael Connors and Ann Garrido, "Doctrinal and Catechetical Preaching," in *A Handbook for Catholic Preaching* (Collegeville, MN: Liturgical Press), 126.

must embrace the worldview of the other culture and learn to think and act in ways that resonate with the other culture.

One solution to these challenges is to study the language of the immigrant community. But just as important, one must study the immigrant's culture. This handbook for the cross-cultural preacher to Latinos meets both of these needs. Although written primarily for cross-cultural preachers to Latinos in the U.S., this resource will be helpful to catechists, parish staffs, lay leaders, parents, and anyone involved in a shared parish. My hope is that pastoral workers will carry it with them as they serve the Hispanic community. It should set off lightbulbs in their minds as they say, "Now I get it. This is why Latinos do it like this." My hope is that this handbook will promote greater understanding and unity in the shared parish. At the same time, I would like to widen this target audience to Hispanic Protestants, educators, and anyone else who tries to preach or teach cross-culturally to Latinos. All these audiences can benefit from this handbook.

I begin Chapter 1 with an example from the early seventeenth century of how to preach cross-culturally. In Chapter 2, I introduce the Hispanic Moment and consider whether the U.S. Catholic Church is ready for it. In Chapter 3, I propose possible responses to the Hispanic Moment. In Chapter 4, I consider the Hispanic worldview and a major symbol. This analysis leads to sacramentality and Hispanic popular religion described in Chapter 5. Chapter 6 explores the historical roots of popular religion. In Chapter 7, I focus on sacramentality and Hispanic preaching. In Chapters 8 and 9, I look at Hispanic sacramentality in the span of a lifetime. Finally, Chapter 10 examines how Latinos express and experience sacramentality over the course of the liturgical year.

1

Cross-Cultural Preaching
One Example from History

Jesus commends the scribe instructed in the kingdom of God who is like the head of a household who brings from his storeroom both the new and the old.[1] Cross-cultural preachers look for wisdom not only in current studies and disciplines, but also study history and look for examples of success in cross-cultural ministry. Studying the history of the Church's efforts at missionary work helps cross-cultural preachers develop a hermeneutic for their particular community. The Jesuit priest Roberto de Nobili was remarkably successful in missionary work in India in the early seventeenth century because he developed a hermeneutic for the people of India at that time.

Born in Rome in 1577, de Nobili came from a wealthy family. His family was one of the most powerful and influential in Rome. He could have chosen a life of wealth and luxury, but he gave it all up and entered the Society of Jesus in 1597.[2] After extensive training in philosophy, logic, linguistics, science, astronomy, metaphysics, ethics, and theology, he was able to follow his desire to become a missionary to India. On May 20, 1605, de Nobili reached Goa and joined the other Jesuit missionaries at St. Stephen's College. After seven months of study, he sailed to the east coast and began missionary work in Madurai,[3] living in southern India for almost forty years (1606–44).[4]

---

[1] Mt. 13:52.

[2] Cody Lorance, "Cultural Relevance and Doctrinal Soundness: The Mission of Roberto de Nobili," *Missiology: An International Review* 33, no. 4 (October 2005): 421.

[3] Victor Raj, "Text and Context in Indian Christian Theology," *Missio Apostolica* 16, no. 2 (November 2008):115.

[4] Francis Clooney, "Roberto de Nobili, Adaptation and the Reasonable Interpretation of Religion, Clooney, *Missiology: An International Review* 18, no. 1 (January 1990): 25.

Upon his arrival in Madurai, de Nobili discovered a big problem. Fr. Goncalo Fernandez, de Nobili's superior at the Jesuit mission at Madurai, had failed to make even one convert after eleven years, despite having good intentions and simplicity of life. The problem was that he had remained so European that the local Hindus considered him unclean and alien.[5]

De Nobili was able to analyze the reasons for Fernandez's failure in Madurai because he had mastered the Tamil language in seven months while studying in Goa, including an immersion experience among the pearl fishers of the Cochin fishery coast.[6] After his arrival in Madurai, de Nobili began to have many conversations with a Tamil language tutor, a Hindu and native of the city. He learned from him that Indian society was a "caste" society. A person's caste was determined by birth, and upward mobility was impossible. One's caste was of utmost importance because it determined social rank, profession, and perceived levels of refinement. Caste rules determined a person's diet, dress, social manners, and relationships.[7] Fernandez's failure to understand this social structure led to a failure of the mission.

Another reason for Fernandez's failure was a linguistic *faux pas*. Words are important vehicles of communication in any culture, but one word in particular proved to be Fernandez's downfall: *parangi*. Cody Lorance describes how this word was understood by the Indians and then how Fernandez understood it:

> *Parangi*, the moniker the Indians had applied to the missionaries, which Fernandez believed simply to be the Tamil word for "Portuguese" (Cronin 1959:45). To the locals, however, the word "signified in the most pejorative sense the polluted, uncultured, contemptuous foreigners and their proselytes. *Parangis* were despised . . . because they ate meat, drank wine (usually to excess), bathed irregularly, wore leather shoes, and ignored the rules of social intercourse" (Neely 1995:47). What made this especially problematic was Fernandez's insistence on using the term as a badge of honor, even using it as a synonym for "Christian." When asking a Hindu to become Christian, he used the phrase, "*Prangui kulam puguda venumo*," which would have been understood as, "Do you want to fall down among the outcaste *Parangis* and become *Parangi*?" (Cronin 1959:45). Naturally, the Hindus began to see Christianity as the religion of the *Parangis* and rejected outright any possibility of conversion due to its inevitable consequence—the loss of caste.[8]

---

5 Clooney, 25.
6 Raj, 115.
7 Lorance, 416.
8 Lorance, 416–17.

De Nobili's linguistic understanding helped him to understand why the Jesuit mission had been a failure up to that point: they fundamentally did not understand the caste structure of Indian society.

What did de Nobili do to remedy this problem? He began the path of *accommodatio*, the missionary method the Jesuits had developed generations prior to de Nobili through Matteo Ricci in China and Alessandro Valignano in Japan.[9] Lorance explains:

> Like Ricci and Valignano, de Nobili sought to remove the barriers that lay between the Hindus of caste and faith in Christ by stripping both the Christian message and the Christian messenger of their respective "cultural 'enclothing'"—that which was strictly European rather than "supracultural revelation from God"—thus leaving only the bare essentials (Kraft 1973:113). He then adopted a variety of forms indigenous to the Indian culture in order to create a culturally relevant or contextualized expression of Christianity.[10]

Source: Grentidez, Public domain, via Wikimedia Commons.

To become intelligible and accepted by Indian society, de Nobili took the radical step of adopting the lifestyle of Hindu holy men, the renunciants known as the *sannyasis*. They took vows of poverty, devoted themselves to prayer, study, asceticism, and training disciples. They wore a cotton cloth draped from their shoulder, walking with painful wooden sandals, and carrying a bamboo staff with seven knots and a gourd of water. They shaved their heads and painted their foreheads with sandalwood paste. Their diet was severe, consisting of one daily meal of rice and herbs. They were highly regarded and sought out for spiritual instruction.[11]

De Nobili not only adopted the lifestyle of a *sannyasis*, but he thoroughly mastered the important languages of Southern India. He mastered the Indian vernacular Tamil so well that later generations referred to him as the "Father of Tamil Prose." By the end of his life, he had written forty works of prose

---

9 Lorance, 417.

10 Lorance, 417.

11 Lorance, 417.

and poetry in Tamil. He also learned and wrote in Telugu and in Sanskrit.¹²

Learning these languages so thoroughly opened the door to Indian thought and culture. De Nobili's language facility helped him in the process of contextualization as he sought to bring the gospel to India. A well-respected Sanskrit scholar Sivadarma granted him access to the secret knowledge of the Hindu religious texts, The Vedas. Sivadarma eventually became the first Brahmin Christian in the Madurai mission.¹³ De Nobili ". . . became familiar with a wide range of popular and technical religious ideas, with popular myths, the legal codes of Manu, etc., and the literature of sectarian Hinduism . . . ."¹⁴

Source: Joanie McMahon.

The method of *accommodatio* involved accepting everything good from Indian culture and rejecting only that which was opposed to the gospel. If an aspect of Indian culture was not against the gospel, it was good and should be respected and retained. This method incorporated aspects of the Madurai Indians into the life of the Church and thereby led to the construction of a culturally relevant expression of Christianity.¹⁵ Lorance cites some examples:

> For example, de Nobili blessed and distributed the sandalwood paste that the Indians used ornamentally to cover the "nakedness" of their foreheads. During the annual festival of Pongal, when the residents of Madurai boiled rice before the idol Vighnes, instead of causing his neophytes the disgrace of not participating in the festivities, he simply replaced the idol with a cross and said a blessing over the rice (Cronin 1959:118–20). Moreover, while de Nobili was careful to teach his congregation that even outcaste Christians deserved love and respect, he essentially upheld the caste system. . . .¹⁶

Accommodatio allowed an Indian to accept Christ while retaining whatever was good in Indian culture of the time.

---

12 Lorance, 418.

13 Lorance, 418.

14 Clooney, 26.

15 Lorance, 419.

16 Lorance, 419.

What was the reaction to de Nobili's method of *accommodatio*? He faced opposition from the start, including from his confrere Fernandez who called his radical methods a denial of the gospel.[17] Despite his early success in winning the people in Madurai for Christ, his Jesuit order, fellow missionaries, and ecclesiastical authorities in both Rome and India opposed his efforts. It's hard to imagine what they were thinking. Could they have been jealous of de Nobili's success? For the most part, they forbade him to accept converts between 1612 and 1623 and forced him to defend his method of *accommodation*. During this period, de Nobili articulated his rationale for his missionary theory by producing three Latin treatises: the *Apology*, the *Narration*, and *Report on Certain Customs of the Indian Nation*.[18] His persecution reached a crescendo with the Goa Conference in 1619 during which he was required to defend his radical methods before his detractors. They accused him of vilest syncretism, of polluting the gospel, and of apostasy.[19] Jesus promises his followers that they will be persecuted for preaching the gospel, but we do not expect that persecution to come from fellow believers.

What results did de Nobili achieve? The evidence shows that de Nobili's efforts resulted in an abundant harvest of Indian disciples of the Lord Jesus Christ. Although his predecessor and elder Fernandez had failed to see one convert after eleven years of work, de Nobili began to see success immediately. By 1610 sixty Hindus had become Christian; two years later that number tripled, and by de Nobili's death in 1656, the total number of Christians surpassed 4,000.[20] de Nobili was able to expand his mission to other cities in India; many Jesuits joined him and succeeded him. They too adopted de Nobili's contextual method of missionary work, and by 1740 the number of Christians in the Indian missions had grown to more than 100,000.[21]

What does the modern cross-cultural preacher learn from de Nobili? Like him, the cross-cultural preacher today must attend to the language of the people, their culture, their history, and must adopt their lifestyle. Two models for cross-cultural preaching are the Incarnation and the Apostle Paul. Fully Jewish as he entered into history, Jesus learned the Jewish language, customs, and worldview. Nevertheless, Jesus' Jewishness and his ministry of proclaiming the good news to the Jewish people were not yet cross-cultural preaching. Only Jesus' encounters with foreigners, such as the centurion

---

17 Lorance, 417.
18 Clooney, 4–5.
19 Lorance, 420.
20 Lorance, 419.
21 Lorance, 421–22.

Roman soldier, the Samaritan woman at the well, and the Syrophoenician woman, were truly cross-cultural preaching.[22] The Apostle Paul's missionary endeavors continued the work of preaching the gospel to people of all cultures in the Mediterranean world. He truly became all things to all people to save some.[23] Likewise, de Nobili sacrificed everything for the gospel of Christ and furthered this mission in the seventeenth century by preaching. Although de Nobili grew up in Italian society and spoke Italian and had a distinct European worldview, he immersed himself so much in Indian culture that by the end of his life he had all but forgotten Italian and had to use an interpreter to write to his family.[24]

Questions for Reflection and Discussion

1. What impresses you about Roberto de Nobili? Why was he successful in his evangelization efforts? If you were to present his life to a stranger, what would you emphasize?

2. In your parish, have you noticed people from a different culture or who speak a different language? What is your reaction? Do you know them? Discuss your interactions with them.

3. Roberto de Nobili followed the Jesuit missionary method of *accommodatio*. What does *accommodatio* mean and are you aware of any modern examples of *accommodatio*?

4. Just as no culture is without goodness, no culture is free of evil. What good did Roberto de Nobili find in Indian culture? What was evil? What is good in U.S. American culture? What is evil?

---

[22] See Mt. 8:5–13 and Mt. 15:21–28.

[23] See 1 Cor. 9:22.

[24] Lorance, 421.

2

The Hispanic Moment

The auxiliary bishop and the vicar for Hispanic ministry invited the priests involved in Hispanic ministry to meet. Seated in a circle, the bishop invited each of us to share what is working well in our parish and what are the significant challenges. As he concluded, he said, "We are in a Hispanic moment now in the U.S. Catholic Church." He did not elaborate what he meant by that statement. He merely stated it.

What is the "Hispanic moment"? In the first chapter, I presented a past moment from the seventeenth century; now I introduce to you a present moment. The U.S. Catholic Church is undergoing a present transformation of becoming predominately Latino. The demographic studies show that she is 43% Latino overall and that 60% of the Catholics under the age of 18 are Latino. The Hispanic moment means not only that the people in the pews are Latinos, but that those involved in leadership and ministries are also increasingly Hispanic.

The U.S. Catholic Church has experienced other moments in her history. In the nineteenth and early twentieth centuries, European Catholics immigrated to the United States of America seeking a better life for their families and communities. These immigration patterns could be characterized as an Irish moment, a German moment, and an Italian or Polish moment. Immigration and the blending of these cultures with American culture produced a rich, vibrant, faith-filled Catholicism. These immigrants formed neighborhoods, baptized their children, built churches and Catholic schools, and fervently practiced their faith in a new land. Governing their parishes, clergy accompanied them and so did religious, who taught in their schools.

What is distinct about the Hispanic moment contrasted with these other moments is the shear size of the Hispanic population in the Catholic Church in the United States. Never has the immigrant population of the U.S.

Catholic Church been so predominantly from one ethnic group. Though not monolithic, this new ethnicity will soon become the majority of Catholics in the United States. Two scholars who have highlighted this transformation are Timothy Matovina and Hosffman Ospino. Both have pointed out these trends and encouraged Catholic leadership to be prepared to respond positively. Has anybody listened to them?

Two members of the U.S. hierarchy have heeded the call from Ospino and Matovina. In his remarks to CALL (Catholic Association of Latino Leaders), now retired Archbishop Charles Chaput stated: "I believe we are at a very powerful 'Latino moment' in our Church—a moment that takes nothing away from the dignity or importance of any other ethnic community, but that simply acknowledges, again, that demography is destiny."[1] He added that the election of Pope Francis is another example of the "Latino moment" and it shouts out an invitation for Catholic Latino leadership.[2]

Archbishop José Gomez has referred to the "Latino moment" on at least two occasions. In an interview with *America* magazine, he spoke of a "Latino moment" underway in the United States. After the election in 2016, it became clear to him how important it is to help the Latino culture make a presence and influence in the U.S.[3] Two years later in the context of the *V Encuentro*, Gomez told NCR, "It is a Latino moment." He was referring to the vast and growing population of Latino Catholics across the U.S.[4]

Scholars too have heeded the call from Ospino and Matovina. Thomas Groome, director of The Church in the 21st Century Center, gathered scholars who have noticed this transformation of the U.S. Catholic Church and produced an issue dedicated to the gift of Latinos to the U.S. Catholic Church. Commenting on their reflections and insights, Groome stated, "As

---

1 Archbishop Chaput, "Archbishop Chaput: We Are at a 'Latino Moment' in the U.S. Church," *National Catholic Register*, Aug. 20, 2014, accessed April 13, 2020, https://www.ncregister.com/daily-news/archbishop-chaput-we-are-at-a-latino-moment-in-the-u.s.-church.

2 Chaput.

3 Archbishop Jose Gomez, "How Can the Church Serve the Hispanic Community at a Time of Rapid Change?" *America*, Oct. 17, 2016, accessed April 13, 2020, https://www.americamagazine.org/faith/2016/10/04/how-can-church-serve-hispanic-community-time-rapid-change. This is a poor translation of the Spanish, in which he says, "*Para mí, está claro que, en este tiempo de elecciones, es importante ayudar a la comunidad latinoamericana a mostrar su presencia e influencia en los Estados Unidos.*" (It is important to help the Latin American community to show her presence and influence in the United States). Mostrar means "to show," "to point out," or "to demonstrate." "To demonstrate or show" her presence and influence is a stronger expression than to "make a presence and influence."

4 Archbishop Jose Gomez, interview by Dan Morris-Young, "'Latino Moment' Declared at Los Angeles *V Encuentro*," *National Catholic Reporter*, Feb. 1, 2018, accessed April 13, 2020, https://www.ncronline.org/news/parish/latino-moment-declared-los-angeles-v-encuentro.

Archbishop José Gomez, Archbishop of Los Angeles. *Source:* Prayitno from Los Angeles, USA, CC BY 2.0, via Wikimedia Commons.

the essays and statistics in this issue of *C21 Resources* attest, now is clearly the 'Hispanic moment' for U.S. Catholicism."[5]

My first experience of the Hispanic moment began with visiting Mexico after my senior year of high school. I had just come to know the Lord through involvement in the Charismatic renewal movement at a neighboring parish. After giving my life to the Lord, I had begun to pray and read the Bible daily. The summer before my freshman year at the University of Notre Dame, I visited a Mexican family. My Spanish improved greatly as did my understanding of Mexican culture. One of the things I noticed right away was the deep devotion of the Mexican people to Our Lady of Guadalupe and to the crucified Christ. I visited the Shrine of the Basilica of Our Lady of Guadalupe in Mexico City and was deeply struck by the piety of the pilgrims. They had deep faith, and they expressed their love and devotion to the Lord in visible ways: by making pilgrimages, genuflecting, praying on their knees, crawling on their knees, prostrating themselves, weeping tears of sadness or joy. Theirs was a faith of emotion and expression that I had not seen before as a Euro-American Catholic from the U.S. This experience of Catholicism is the origin of the deep faith that Hispanic immigrants bring to the U.S. This

---

5 Thomas Groome, "Ever Becoming a 'Catholic' Church," *C21 Resource*, Spring 2016: 1. Accessed April 13, 2020. https://www.bc.edu/content/dam/files/top/church21/pdf/BC-Share/C21%20SPRING%202016%20Resources_%20The%20Treasure%20of%20Hispanic%20Catholicism.pdf.

deep faith deepened my newborn life of faith. My faith at this point was like a new plant budding forth out of the ground. The Hispanic piety served as water, sunlight, and fertilizer for the fragile sapling I was trying to cultivate.

That experience occurred in 1982. Fast-forwarding fourteen years later to 1996. When I entered the seminary, the Hispanic moment was happening all around me. A large group of seminarians was Latino and I became friends with many of them. We played soccer, attended Mass and prayers, went to class, and ate meals together. Those relationships helped me to improve my Spanish and just as important to understand Hispanic culture. My daily life of interacting with Latino seminarians opened my eyes to see concrete evidence of the Hispanic moment: the Church's leadership in the U.S. was being developed right before my eyes in these Latinos. I did not notice, however, many Anglo seminarians becoming proficient in Spanish language or Hispanic culture. They would take one or two Spanish courses and be done with their requirements. They were not ready for ministry in shared parishes with a large Hispanic population. This seems to be common in many seminaries and local churches and is cause for concern. Why were Anglo-American seminarians not paying attention to the Hispanic moment?

On July 2, 1999, the archbishop ordained me a deacon and assigned me to a parish on the West coast. This year of ministry deepened my experience of the Hispanic moment. In contrast to many of the Anglo parishes, Latinos filled the church for Sunday Mass, including the 1:00 pm liturgy, which was often standing-room only. I began my life as a preacher preparing homilies in Spanish for a captive audience. In a friendly competition with other seminarians, I remember setting a record number of Baptisms with over 200 baptisms in a year. Another memorable moment was the first experience of *mañanitas* at 4:30 am for Our Lady of Guadalupe. The church was completely filled with people standing from wall to wall. Because of so many people, the church was hot. I remember sweating but being so thrilled and excited to be part of such a popular and dramatic moment—truly a Hispanic moment.

Witnessing a filled church for Sunday masses, over 200 baptisms, and an overflowing crowd for Our Lady of Guadalupe was a contrast to what was happening in the parish I grew up in. My parents are still faithful members of this parish in the Detroit area. The neighborhood I grew up in has changed; all my brothers and sisters have grown up, become educated, obtained jobs, married, and moved elsewhere to begin raising their families. They have moved to the outer suburbs of Detroit looking for good schools for their children and safe neighborhoods. The populations that replaced them are mostly Muslim immigrants from the Middle East. The parish reflects the changes in the demographics of the neighborhood. Now the church membership is parishioners the age of my eighty-year-old parents. This catholic parish is literally dying. On the other hand, parishes where my brothers and sister now live are well-attended. This anecdotal history of my parent's parish helps us to understand the transformation of the U.S. Catholic Church. Some parishes are dying while others are growing. Immigration seems to be the leading factor causing this change.

The Hispanic moment involves a concern for social justice. I would like to share with you the following homily on Jesus' encounter with the Samaritan woman to illustrate this connection to the social teaching of the Church:

> In late January 2008, José Luis went to work as usual in a vegetable processing plant in North Portland. However, that day a surprise happened. ICE officials raided the plant and arrested all the workers suspected of being illegals. Maria, his wife, and their three children were surprised to receive a phone call later that day saying that José Luis was in prison. Immediately the question arose for the family. How are we going to survive here in the U.S. if our major breadwinner is in prison? Of course, the common narrative on talk radio and on the street was antagonistic: "You're Mexican. You're illegal. You're a criminal. You broke the law. You came here illegally. You overstayed your visa. Your children are being educated here because of my taxes. You don't pay taxes. We don't like you and we want you to leave. You should be deported."
>
> Like José Luis and his family, the Samaritan woman also experienced antagonism. She was a Samaritan, and the Samaritans were despised by the Jews. In the minds of the Jewish people, the Samaritans were the religious apostates. The Samaritans were the heretics. When she confronts Jesus at the well, she expects opposition and disparagement. When Jesus asks her for a drink, she responds, "How is it that you a Jew, ask a drink of me, a woman of Samaria?" (Jn. 4:9). She expects to be ignored. That was custom. There is an underlying tension in this initial encounter due to history, culture, and race.
>
> Jesus too is aware of the conflict. He doesn't flee it, doesn't deny it, doesn't ignore it. Rather, he enters into it. Against custom, the Jewish man Jesus engages the woman in conversation. He has a dialogue with her. He deals with the differences. The woman says: "Our fathers worshiped on this mountain, and you say that in Jerusalem is the place where men ought to worship" (Jn. 4:20). Jesus responds, "You worship what you do not know: we worship what we know, for salvation is from the Jews" (Jn. 4:22). Jesus breaks through the antagonism between Jews and Samaritans and brings freedom to the woman, freedom from bondage to sin. After this encounter with Jesus, she goes to the Samaritan village and says, "Come, see a man who told me all that I ever did. Can this be the Christ?" (Jn. 4:39). She

becomes an evangelist. The gospel writer John says, "Many Samaritans believed in him because of the woman's testimony" (Jn. 4:39).

After the ICE raid, I preached to the Anglo community: "How do we respond to this human tragedy? This isn't just a story we read upon the front page of *The Oregonian,* [Portland's newspaper]. Rather we know José Luis and his family. They aren't just names without faces. They're our parishioners." I preached on the corporal works of mercy that weekend: "We are called to feed the hungry, shelter the homeless, visit prisoners." We took up a second collection. We helped Jose Luis hire an immigration attorney and get out of prison. We also helped the family pay for rent as they had no income during this time. We took action.

"As we continue this Lenten season, ask yourself: Who is José Luis in my parish or community and what am I doing to free him?"

I preached this homily on social justice to a shared parish with a large Latino population. Teaching, preaching, and practicing social justice is an effective way to integrate Latino immigrants and Euro-American parishioners. The principles of solidarity and a preferential option for the poor call all Catholics of all ethnicities to work for the dignity of every human being. This family needed help because of the immigration raid. Both the Hispanic community and the Euro-Americans responded generously to this need by giving to a second collection for the family in need. Integration and unity occur when the shared parish focuses on living the gospel in practical ways.

Source: Joanie McMahon.

I would like to share two more experiences of the Hispanic moment. When I lived on the West Coast, I used my continuing education money to attend the LA Congress, the largest religious education conference in the U.S. Catholic Church occurring every year in Anaheim, California. The first time I went to the Congress I was immediately struck by the large crowds of Latinos. Experts in Hispanic ministry from all over the world visited this conference to address the large Latino crowds. Their enthusiasm, warmth, humor, love, joy, and love for the Lord and his Blessed Mother were palpable. Walking past the conference booths and seeing all the vendors with Hispanic materials for catechesis, Bible, evangelization, and parish leadership showed me a clear response to the Hispanic moment. Later, in the gathering of 20,000 Catholics for Mass, the Hispanic presence was visible and boisterous. One could describe their presence at that liturgy as full, conscious, and active participation.

Another large gathering of Latinos also demonstrated the Hispanic moment. In Dallas in 2018, Hispanic leaders and faithful met in Dallas for the fifth *Encuentro*. The first *Encuentro* in 1972 served the purpose of developing a pastoral plan for Latinos in the U.S. In the decades that followed, Hispanic leaders met for three more *Encuentros* to continue this endeavor.[6] Meeting with so many Latinos at one place in Dallas was a powerful experience of the Body of Christ. I travelled there with a staff member and a young Latina parishioner. We were part of a delegation of Hispanic leaders from

Source: Photo by Igor Rodrigues on Unsplash.

6 For a history of the *Encuentros*, see Timothy Matovina's *Latino Catholicism*, 76–86.

our Archdiocese. Bishops and lay people addressed the large crowds at both talks and liturgies. I was impressed by the young Latinos who expressed their desire to have the Church accompany them in their growth as Christians. They know they cannot do it alone; they need our help. Like my first experience of a wall-to-wall filled church at my first *mañanitas*, this experience of the *V Encuentro* in Dallas renewed my faith and deepened my hope. The Catholic Church in the U.S. is alive! Jesus is alive! Mary his mother is alive!

My concluding vignette is a meeting of the archbishop with Hispanic ministers in the archdiocese. The office of Latino ministry organized this prayer and listening event as part of the preparation for the archdiocesan synod. The welcome was immediately followed by the archbishop addressing the reason we were gathering: to listen to the Lord and to one another, and then to share our insights with him. That's what we did. At the end of the session the Archbishop invited us all to share our thoughts. After most of the other members voiced their thoughts, the microphone came to me. I was praying all the time that I would have the right words to say. Here's what I said:

> Archbishop, I thank you for your leadership of the Archdiocese. The strengths of my parish include marriage and family life, faith formation, and evangelization. The weaknesses are youth, young adult ministry, and social justice ministry. I have wanted to hire Latino workers to meet these needs but have been unable to fund these positions because of the lack of resources. Might I suggest, your excellency, that a portion of the CSA (Catholic Service Appeal) be designated to provide resources so that parishes like mine can hire workers. We need these funds because we are not a wealthy parish like the parishes in the suburbs. My concern is that we are not investing resources in the areas where the church is growing: the shared parishes with large Latino communities. Your excellency, when I look at the poster of the seminarians from our Archdiocese, there are fifty-two seminarians, but not one Latino on that poster. Archbishop, my fear is that we are in a Hispanic moment and not ready for it.

Questions for Reflection and Discussion

1. What is the Hispanic Moment? How do you notice it in your parish and in society? Has your experience of the Hispanic Moment been positive or negative?
2. What struck you about the author's experiences of the Hispanic Moment? Why?
3. The Hispanic Moment involves social justice. Two themes of Catholic Social Teaching are solidarity and a preferential option for the poor. How do these two principles apply to the Hispanic moment in your parish and diocese?
4. The Hispanic moment is upon us. Discuss the level of engagement with it in your life, your parish, and your diocese.

3

The Hispanic Moment and a Theology of Communion

Are we ready for the Hispanic moment we are currently encountering? I would like to use this question as a springboard for a consideration of Hispanic community and a theology of communion. I have two experiences to share which illustrate two different responses to the Hispanic moment.

The first occurred when I was a newly ordained priest. After Mass, a Mexican family approached and asked me if I would go to the hospital to anoint their father who was dying. At the seminary, I learned that if someone was dying, I was to drop everything, go, and show the dying person the love of the Christ and the Church. So, that's what I did. A few weeks later, I got a call that the Mexican father had died, and the family was arranging the funeral with the parochial vicar of another parish. I called to tell him I would help as needed. I explained the Mexican custom of a novena of rosary prayers for the deceased. His response: "That is not the way to celebrate a funeral. They are here now, so they have to do things the way we do them in the United States."

The second example was a young, newly ordained priest whose first assignment was a shared parish with a large Hispanic ministry. He had taken several good Spanish courses in the seminary and was determined to become fluent. He also had the good fortune of having spent a summer in Mexico. This newly ordained man had the good quality of understanding the importance of relationships. He maintained his friendships with the family he had stayed with in Mexico, even inviting the mother of the family to his ordination. He was responsible for coordinating ministry to the sick and dying in a shared parish with a large Latino population. Although he was

Anglo American, he showed God's merciful love to the Hispanic community, responding immediately to an emergency call from a Latino parishioner.

Are we ready for the Hispanic moment? The answer is yes and no. The second priest was clearly ready. He had prepared in the seminary, worked hard to learn Spanish and acquire greater understanding of Hispanic culture, and even made sacrifices to travel to Mexico and learn. The first priest was in no way ready. He was closed to the possibility of cross-cultural preaching and ministry and unable to meet the needs of at least some of those in his pastoral care. He is a portrait of someone who is not prepared for the Hispanic moment.

It's worth asking what is holding him back. Fear of learning Spanish? Fear of having to change? A feeling of superiority? A lack of charity? Fear of a Hispanic invasion? A big obstacle to meeting the U.S. Catholic Church's Hispanic moment is an attitude that Latino immigrants must assimilate and become like Euro-Americans in all things. This stems from the notion that Hispanic immigrants will assimilate into the melting pot of the United States of America and become thoroughly Euro-American, leaving their Spanish language and customs from their countries of origin behind them.

Those holding this assimilation viewpoint expect that Hispanic immigration will follow the same dynamic as European Catholic immigrants from the great century of immigration from 1820 to 1920. Matovina, however,

Pope Francis prepares the Church for the Hispanic Moment. *Source:* Tânia Rêgo/ABr, CC BY 3.0 BR, via Wikimedia Commons.

illustrates how this new wave of immigration is different. He gives seven reasons: the physical proximity of the countries, the continuous flow of immigrants, poverty, racism, urbanization, Church teaching on cultural adaptation in ministry, and the persistence of Popular Religion.[1] I will focus on the first two reasons to highlight the difference of today's Latino immigrants. European Catholic immigrants from the great wave of immigration from 1820 to 1920 had to travel by boat across the ocean. Most immigrant Latinos today come from countries closer to the U.S. Moreover, contact between the country of origin and the U.S. is more frequent for today's Latinos than for the immigrants who crossed the ocean. Spanish television keeps Latinos entertained and informed about what is occurring in their home countries.[2] In contrast to those in the nineteenth century, today's immigrants can pick up their cellphones and communicate easily with their families in Guatemala. A Latino mother can make a zoom call and see her loved ones in Mexico. Improvements in technology have made communication instantaneous.

Also unlike the first waves of European Catholic immigration, today's Latino immigration is marked by a continuous flow of immigrants. The legislation of 1924 curtailed further immigration of Germans, Italians, Polish, Irish, and other Catholic immigrants from Europe. This dynamic accelerated the acceptance of U.S. cultural values and led to the assimilation of these immigrants. In contrast, Hispanic immigration shows no signs of abating, despite efforts to restrict immigration.[3] "A steady flow of new arrivals continuously reenforces language and culture and is a second important difference between today's Latinos and yesterday's European Catholic Immigrants."[4]

The assimilation worldview is not the gospel. Paul becomes all things to all people so that some may be saved (1 Cor. 9:22). He enters Greek culture, preaches the gospel, converts the Gentiles, and brings them into the Church, the Body of Christ. A new humanity is created when the gospel enters into this pagan culture and changes it in Christ: the resulting culture is a blend of the gospel with the pagan culture in a way that redeems and purifies it. Jesus preaches cross-culturally when he meets the Samaritan woman at the well and offers her living water. Jesus does not dismiss her and say she must assimilate, rather he meets her where she is and offers her new life in the gospel. Yes, fear and anxiety accompany the reception of the Hispanic

---

[1] Timothy Matovina, "No Melting Pot in Sight," in *Perspectivas: Hispanic Ministry*, eds. Deck, Tarango, and Matovina (Kansas City: Sheed & Ward, 1995), 35–39.
[2] Matovina, "No Melting Pot in Sight," 36.
[3] Matovina, "No Melting Pot in Sight," 36.
[4] Matovina, "No Melting Pot in Sight," 36.

moment. Fear that the Latinos will "take over." Fear that Euro-Americans will become the minority. Fear of conflict. Anxiety is also present. We worry about having to celebrate Mass in Spanish or preside at *quinceañeras*. We worry about immigrant Latinos not contributing to the collection to balance the parish budget.

Rather than responding to this moment with fear and anxiety, a better response flows from envisioning the Hispanic moment as a gift to the U.S. Catholic Church. This gift is foundational in that it concerns the Church at her deepest identity. I maintain that the most important part of the Hispanic moment is the development of a communion ecclesiology for Church renewal. To explain what I mean by this claim, I will briefly define it before considering the historical development of this theology.

Communion ecclesiology is an understanding of the Church in which relationships are emphasized: among the persons of the Trinity, among human beings and God, among members of the Communion of Saints, and among bishops throughout the world. This approach attempts to move beyond a mere juridical or institutional church understanding and instead emphasizes the mystical, sacramental, and historical dimensions of the Church. It highlights the relationship between the Church universal and local churches.[5]

The communion of saints highlights communion ecclesiology in which relationships are paramount. *Source:* © José Luiz Bernardes Ribeiro / CC BY-SA 4.0.

5 Dennis Doyle, *Communion Ecclesiology* (Maryknoll, New York: Orbis Books, 2000), 12.

A communion ecclesiology or theology of communion finds its roots in the work of Johann Adam Moehler, a nineteenth century professor at the University of Tubingen. He developed a theology with a focus on the unity of the church in which he set forth a more mystical understanding. This understanding served as the basis for a later communion ecclesiology.[6] Moehler's thought is further developed in the work of a contemporary Hispanic theologian Roberto Goizueta. "Like Moehler, Goizueta sees that universality needs to be grasped by recognizing communalities in and through particularities."[7] To illustrate this idea, Goizueta gives the example of a man and marriage. The way a man comes to understand the universal of marriage is not by marrying as many women as possible. Rather, by entering into a lifelong relationship with one particular woman, a man comes to understand the universal of marriage. Understanding of the particular leads to an understanding of the universal.[8]

Goizueta's focus on relationships is the main connection between Goizueta's theology and a theology of communion. Dennis Doyle states: "Like Johann Adam Moehler … Goizueta places his initial emphasis on the relationships among God and human beings that exist within local liturgical communities. The unity in the church is first of all a bondedness in love that values rather than erases diversity."[9] Goizueta begins with the local church made up of particular people before moving to the Church universal. The Hispanic moment brings great diversity to the Church both with the Spanish language and accompanying dialects and with new cultures and customs. A unity in love is what holds this diversity together. Perhaps the reason that the U.S. Catholic Church is not ready for the Hispanic moment is a lack of charity in our parishes. We fundamentally do not love our neighbor when we fail to love and welcome immigrants and value their languages, cultures, and customs. As I write this, the movie *A Beautiful Day in the Neighborhood*, starring Tom Hanks, is playing at the theaters. Mr. Rogers's efforts to connect with children had a lasting beneficial effect. Just as Mr. Rogers sought to be "neighbor" to younger generations, so too cross-cultural preachers attempt to be "neighbor" to those who are culturally different.

---

6   James Empereur and Eduardo Fernandez, *La Vida Sacra: Contemporary Hispanic Sacramental Theology* (Lanham, Maryland: Rowman & Littlefield, 2006), 26.

7   Empereur and Fernandez, 26.

8   Roberto Goizueta, *Caminemos con Jesus: Toward a Hispanic/Latino Theology of Accompaniment* (Maryknoll, NY: Orbis Books, 1995), 97.

9   Dennis Doyle, "Communion Ecclesiology on the Borders," in *Theology: Expanding the Borders* (Mystic, CT: Twenty Third Publications, 1998), 208.

The Congregation for the Doctrine of the Faith (CDF) produced a letter to the bishops of the Catholic Church entitled *On Some Aspects of the Church Understood as Communion*.[10] The strongest points of convergence between the CDF's document on the Church as Communion and Goizueta lie in communion ecclesiology, their emphasis on the relational aspects of the Catholic faith, and their ability to link the particular communities with the universal elements of God and the shared tradition.[11] "It's all about relationships" is a phrase repeatedly uttered in this preaching manual. Although it applies to Hispanic ministry in all its forms, it also applies to communion ecclesiology. God is a Trinity of Persons, a community. The Father, the Son, and the Holy Spirit call and gather a people, and make their home in them (John:14:23). By the outpouring of the Holy Spirit, they become the Body of Christ, the Church. Just as God is relationships, so too human beings find their origin and fulfillment in relationships with God and with other human beings. Communion ecclesiology focuses on relationships to understand the nature of the Church.

Goizueta's contribution to communion ecclesiology shows how the Hispanic community serves as a living, breathing, acting example of communion

The presence of Latinos in our parishes is a fully alive example of communion ecclesiology calling us to unity in diversity. *Source:* Joanie McMahon.

10 Congregation for the Doctrine of the Faith, *On Some Aspects of the Church Understood as Communion*, 1992.

11 Doyle, "Communion Ecclesiology on the Borders," 215.

ecclesiology. Communion ecclesiology is "enfleshed" in the Hispanic Catholic community. Abstract theology comes to life when one ministers in the Hispanic community: unity in diversity is present and the communal precedes the individual. In addition, the Hispanic community's presence in the Church serves as a corrective to U.S. consumer culture focused on the desires of the solitary individual. Goizueta's approach is provocative:

> Goizueta sees the Trinity as representing the communal nature of God; "personhood" is not prior to community but is achieved within it. The model holds true also for human relationships. Goizueta argues against the tendency of the dominant U.S. culture to see individuality as a primary reality that exists prior to any relationships. In Goizueta's U.S. Hispanic perspective, community precedes individuality. Authentic individuality is achieved only within the context of a community which precedes one and from which one draws one's identity. True freedom is found not in a struggle to be a completely autonomous self-made person, but only in relationships.... Interrelatedness as persons lies at the very heart of reality.[12]

The Trinity exists from all eternity. The Father eternally is in relation to his Son; the Son is eternally in relation to the Father; and the Holy Spirit is the love exchanged eternally between the Father and the Son. This dynamic shows the personhood of God and the prior nature of community.

If this communal nature is true of the Trinity of persons, it is also true of human relationships. We are in relationship from the moment of our birth. Our parents teach and nurture us. We grow up in community and through relationships with family and friends we mature and grow. Only by giving ourselves to others in family and community do we reach fulfillment as human beings. In this way, relationships are not a hindrance to freedom, but rather a way that human beings exercise freedom and reach fulfillment. One Latino woman pastor commented on this aspect of preaching to Latinos: "When I'm referring to identity in a sermon for a Hispanic group, somehow I have to bring in the family theme or some family focus there, because that's what our identity's based on."[13] The source of personal identity in the family is why Confession often becomes a recitation of the sins of the rest of the family. It is hard for Latinos to distance themselves from their families whether in confessing their sins or seeking counsel from a priest.

Although a study of individualism would be beyond the scope of this preaching manual, American culture is characterized by it. It almost takes

---

12 Doyle, "Communion Ecclesiology on the Borders," 208–9.

13 James Nieman and Thomas Rogers, *Preaching to Every Pew: Cross-Cultural Strategies* (Minneapolis: Fortress Press, 2001), 34.

travel abroad and experience of a communal culture to recognize this worldview in ourselves. A recent trip to Colombia and a stay with a Colombian extended family brought this home to me. I shared an apartment with the grandmother, her two daughters, a son, and their niece. Everybody was concerned about everyone else. If we went out to eat, we always thought about those who stayed home and purchased extra food and brought it to them afterward. We also shared expenses, taking turns to pay for the food and travel. The Hispanic moment has the potential to transform the U.S. Catholic Church to be more in conformity with the gospel.

My concern that we are in a Hispanic moment and not ready for it is an attempt to bring about *metanoia* in the U.S. Catholic Church. *Metanoia* is conversion: a turning around of one's direction and mind. The two examples of the two newly ordained priests with which I opened this chapter show *metanoia* on the part of the second and the need for *metanoia* on the part of the first. He was fundamentally opposed to *metanoia* called for in the Hispanic moment. The conversion called for involves the willingness to enter into the worldview of the other. The next chapter explores the worldview of the Hispanic immigrants around one major symbol.

Questions for Reflection and Discussion

1. Contrast the two priests' reaction to the Hispanic moment. If they represent a spectrum from negative to positive, where do you find yourself? Why?

2. What is a theology of communion and how can this theology help us to understand the Church?

3. Talk about individualism and its effects upon you, your family, parish, and community.

4. How might Hispanic culture be an effective remedy for U.S. consumer culture focused on the individual?

4

Worldviews and U.S. Latinos

To preach effectively from one culture to another requires that preachers understand the worldview of the people to whom they preach. N. T. Wright, the noted biblical scholar, has developed a methodology for understanding the worldview of another culture, and this method has produced fruitful scriptural scholarship. By using this methodology, preachers attempting to preach cross-culturally to Latinos in the U.S. today can enter into their worldview. By following N. T. Wright's methodology for one key symbol in the U.S. Hispanic worldview, this chapter provides a foundation upon which the cross-cultural preacher can build.

The worldviews of a people compose the way in which they order reality. They involve the presuppositional, pre-cognitive, stage of a culture or a society.[1] They consist of the symbols, the stories, the praxis, and the questions of a society. Wright describes them as follows: "Worldviews are thus the basic stuff of human existence, the lens through which the world is seen, the blueprint for how one should live in it, and above all the sense of identity and place which enables human beings to be what they are."[2] All cultures and societies have worldviews and for the cross-cultural preachers, they must learn to move from their own worldview to one that is foreign to them.

Wright says that worldviews characteristically do four things. First, "worldviews provide the stories through which human beings view reality."[3]

---

1 N. T. Wright, *The New Testament and the People of God*, Vol. 1, Christian Origins and the Question of God (Minneapolis: Fortress Press, 1992), 122. See also N.T. Wright, *Paul and the Faithfulness of God*, Vol. 4, Christian Origins and the Question of God (Minneapolis: Fortress Press, 2013), 24–36.

2 Wright, 124.

3 Wright, 123.

Narrative thus becomes one way of catching a glimpse of the worldview of a people. Second, worldviews determine the basic questions of human existence: "who are we, where are we, what is wrong, and what is the solution?"[4] These are basic questions all cultures attempt to answer. Third, the stories and their answers to these basic questions all express themselves in cultural symbols. These can be both artifacts and events, such as festivals and family gatherings.[5] Fourth, worldviews include praxis, which is a way-of-being-in-the-world. The answer to the basic question, "What is the solution?" necessarily leads to action. By looking at an individual's actions, the real shape of that person's worldview can be revealed.[6]

When applied to the Hispanic culture in the U.S. in 2022, Wright's methodology provides cross-cultural preachers a way of crossing the chasm between two cultures: that is, the dominant Euro-American culture and the immigrant Latino culture. Cross-cultural preachers gain much insight by systematically examining each of the four categories. Without claiming to do a comprehensive study of Hispanic culture in the U.S. in 2022, this chapter will focus on one of its central symbols, the story behind this symbol, the praxis as a response to this story, and the answers given by this story, symbol, and praxis.

The two central symbols for Latinos in the U.S. in 2022 are the crucified Christ and his sorrowful mother.[7] Although the Virgin Mary is honored under different titles in different Hispanic countries, she is widely honored as Our Lady of Guadalupe in the U.S. because most Latinos in the U.S. are of Mexican origin. Because of the centrality of this symbol in the Hispanic imagination, the most important first step to care for Latinos is to display the image of Our Lady of Guadalupe in the parish church. Showing this image in a prominent place allows the faithful to come and greet her as they would their mother. They say "good morning" and "goodbye" to her with much affection and emotion. They love to light a candle and say a pray to *la Morenita*, "the little brown-skinned one." Mary appeared in

Source: Public domain.

---

4 Wright, 123.

5 Wright, 123.

6 Wright, 123.

7 Matovina, *Latino Catholicism*, 166.

sixteenth century Mexico in the form of an indigenous young woman, and she was *en cinta* (literally "belted"), the sign that she was pregnant, carrying the true king in her womb.[8]

Why did this symbol capture the minds and hearts of a whole people and nation? The history of the conversion of Mexico was dependent upon the revealing of this image to the indigenous people. The early missionaries were largely unsuccessful in their evangelization efforts. It was only when Juan Diego brought the *tilma*, his cloak, with image of the Virgin Mary, to Bishop Zumarraga, and he began to venerate and display the image to the people that the conversions to Christ and the Catholic Church increased rapidly and in record number. Why? The image of Our Lady of Guadalupe was a picture of the gospel in a way that the indigenous people could understand and receive it. It was the gospel at their level and in their language. The indigenous people worshiped the sun, and Mary is blocking but not extinguishing the sun.[9] The true one to worship is in Mary's womb: he is the source of all life. He is the light. The image of Our Lady of Guadalupe harmonized the good of the indigenous people and their culture with the good news of the gospel. This central symbol is an example of inculturation of the gospel.

The symbol leads to the story of Guadalupe, which reveals Emmanuel, "God is with us" (Matthew 1:23).[10] One notes three striking characteristics in this narrative. First, God comes to a broken people in despair, gives them hope, and begins to build them anew. The indigenous people were broken by the Spanish Conquistadores with the final battle of conquest on Aug. 13, 1521. Their temples were destroyed, their gods defeated, and their women violated.[11] They were a defeated people in despair. Nevertheless, God does not abandon them; he sends them Mary to bring them the gospel, renew their hope, and rebuild them as a people. Second, Juan Diego is central to the narrative, and he is one with whom the indigenous can identify. He is a humble indigenous man. The terms he calls himself shows how God chooses the lowly to do great things. He doubts his ability to be the appropriate messenger to the bishop saying, "I am a [porter's] rope, I am a backframe, a tail, a wing, a man of no importance."[12] Juan Diego obeys the Virgin, and God does wonders. Third, Our Lady of Guadalupe reveals the reason she wants

---

8 Kenneth Davis, "Cross-cultural preaching," in *Preaching and Culture in Latino Congregations* (hereafter referred to as *PCLC*), ed. Kenneth Davis and Jorge Presmanes (Chicago: Liturgy Training Publications, 2000), 50.

9 Virgilio Elizondo, "Our Lady of Guadalupe as a Cultural Symbol," in *Mestizo Worship: A Pastoral Approach to Liturgical Ministry*, ed. Virgilio Elizondo and Timothy Matovina (Collegeville: Liturgical Press, 1998), 39–42.

10 New American Bible (NAB).

11 Elizondo, 38.

12 Victor Alvarez, "Preaching to Generation X," in *PCLC*, 127–28.

Source: Joanie McMahon.   Basilica of Guadalupe, Mexico. *Source:* Unknown author, public domain, via Wikimedia Commons.

a temple built by the bishop. It is so that in it she "can show and give forth all my love, compassion, help, and defense to all the inhabitants of this land ... to hear their lamentations and remedy their miseries, pain, and sufferings."[13] She wants to be the mother of the indigenous people. The mother is a revered figure in Hispanic culture, responsible for handing on the culture, traditions, and the faith practices.[14] This reverence is undoubtedly related to the veneration of Our Lady of Guadalupe.

Praxis revolves around the December 12th feast day of Our Lady of Guadalupe. The day starts with *mañanitas* early in the morning, often at 4:00 am or 5:00 am. Thousands of U.S. Latinos attend church on this day to honor Our Lady. The custom is to sing "good morning" to her and ask her protection for oneself and one's family. Flowers, a profound symbol of the divine, are bought, carried, and placed before the image of our Lady. Flowers and music were supreme ways of communication with the divine for the indigenous people of Mexico. The apparition to Juan Diego began with music and reached its culmination with flowers, the sign of life beyond life.[15]

On a practical level, this feast day creates some interesting challenges if it occurs on a Saturday or Sunday. Does a parish adapt its weekend Masses to accommodate the overflow of visitors? Is Mary shown special honor by proper prayers for the feast day of Our Lady of Guadalupe? What happens to Advent liturgical prayers? I would favor praying the liturgical prayers for

---

[13] Elizondo, 40.
[14] Raul Gomez, "Preaching the Ritual Masses among Latinos," in *PCLC*, 111.
[15] Elizondo, 42.

Our Lady of Guadalupe as she is the reason Latinos flock to the church on December 12th. Analogously, if a wedding occurs during Lent, the proper for a wedding takes precedent over the Lenten prayers. All these issues are confronted by a parish with a large Latino population who flock to the church on December 12th. The overflowing crowds bring to mind the many inactive Latino Catholics who may live in the vicinity of the parish.

The church is left open the entire day and the faithful come throughout the day to offer prayers and spend time with *La Morenita*. Some parishes offer midday prayer services. A solemn Mass followed by a celebration of food and festivity in the parish hall conclude the evening. Often families eat special foods, such as tamales, to celebrate this festive day.

How does the Guadalupe event answer the basic human questions of the Hispanic person in the U.S.? Recall that these concerns involve "who we are, where we are, what is wrong, and what is the solution?" The answer to the first question of "who we are?" is that Latinos in the U.S. are mostly Mexican American immigrants. There is a line in one of the popular hymns sung to the Virgin of Tepeyac: "*Ser mexicano es ser guadalupano*," which translates, "To be Mexican is to be a devotee of Our Lady of Guadalupe." It is often said that all Mexican Americans are Catholic on December 12th. Even though they may have left the Catholic Church and regularly attend a Protestant church, they return to the Catholic parish for the annual celebration of the Guadalupe event. Some Mexicans who have joined Pentecostals and other groups, however, condemn Guadalupan devotion as Catholic superstition.[16]

"Who are we and where are we?" In addition to being *guadalupanos*, Latinos are also immigrants in a foreign land. They have left their homeland in search of a better life for themselves and their children. The presidential election in the U.S. in 2016 and the uncertainty caused by the rhetoric of the campaign against Mexican immigrants caused much fear in the Hispanic community.[17] Latinos are foreigners in exile. The biblical narratives of exile are powerful because they speak to the reality of the Hispanic experience of leaving their homeland and being a foreigner in a new land. Abraham, humanity's father in faith, experiences similar displacement when God called him from his homeland to journey to a new land and to found a new people (Genesis 12:1–9). Mary and Joseph, too, experienced exile as they fled with

---

[16] For an introduction to the discussion on Catholic and Latino Protestants and their differing views on the Virgin Mary, including her manifestation as Our Lady of Guadalupe, see Carmen Nako-Fernandez, "From Pájaro to Paraclete: Retrieving the Spirit of God in the Company of Mary," in *Building Bridges, Doing Justice: Constructing a Latino/a Ecumenical Theology*, ed. Orlando Espin (Maryknoll, NY: Orbis Books, 2009), 13–20.

[17] Mila Koumpilova and Miguel Otarola, "'Constant Fear' as Immigrants Brace for Life under Trump," *Star Tribune*, Monday Nov. 14, 2016.

the newborn Jesus to the land of Egypt to protect him from evil rulers who sought to murder him (Matthew 2:13–15).

"What is wrong?" Latinos are rejected by the dominant culture that treats them as problems and discriminates against them because of the color of their skin or the way they speak.[18] They also experience family breakdown: marriages often are marked by verbal fights and sometimes domestic violence.[19] Pornography is pervasive as is an overly sensual media culture. Adultery is not uncommon among both sexes. Parents often do not know how to raise their children. Children are often confused as they try to figure out who they are. They inhabit two cultural and linguistic worlds: the Latino heritage and Spanish language of their parents and the surrounding American culture and English language. Like other households of poor and middle-income families, Hispanic parents also experience economic hardships as they try to pay high housing and rental costs, pay off credit card debt, and provide for a family of two or more children. Often fathers and mothers must work two or three jobs to pay the bills, and this practice leads to the children often lacking supervision. Families adapt to this reality by having the older children care for the younger children while mom and dad are working. These financial pressures were true before the outbreak of the Covid-19 virus in March and April of 2020, and the pandemic has only exacerbated the economic stress. The lockdown of the society and the economy have caused much unemployment in the Hispanic community because the majority of their work is in service industries, such as restaurants, hotels, landscaping, healthcare support, as well as agriculture and construction. Regarding their children, the dropout rate for Latino youth in school is high, and teenage pregnancies (and abortions) are not uncommon.[20] In summary, what they love most—their families—experience the ravages of sin. This sin and their status as undocumented workers are the most fundamental problems.[21]

What is the solution? Just as Our Lady of Guadalupe came to a broken, indigenous people and led them to the religion of the true king, she can help Latinos today with their family breakdown and immigration difficulties. She can be their refuge in the middle of a pandemic. She can help them to restore their marriages, to bring harmony to their homes, to be good parents to their

---

[18] Virgilio Elizondo, *Galilean Journey: The Mexican American Promise* (Maryknoll: Orbis Books, 2003), 26.

[19] Nichole Flores, "Latina/o Families: Solidarity and the Common Good," in *Journal of the Society of Christian Ethics* 33, no. 2 (2013): 61.

[20] Centers for Disease Control and Prevention (CDC), "About Teen Pregnancy," November 15, 2021, https://www.cdc.gov/teenpregnancy/about/index.htm.

[21] These are the author's observations after having worked in pastoral ministry among U.S. Latinos for twenty-one years between 2000 and 2022.

children, to assist them to be healthy, to have their economic needs provided for, and to support them to adapt to a new country and language. She is their mother, and she cares for them. The solution is to become *Guadalupanos*: Latinos should become more ardent devotees of our Lady of Guadalupe. Anything the Church can do to foster that is worth pursuing.

Questions for Reflection and Discussion

1. Have you heard the story of Our Lady of Guadalupe before? What do you find interesting about it?
2. What are the stories that give meaning to your life?
3. What are the praxis and symbols you see in American culture? How do they differ from Hispanic culture?
4. How do you answer the important questions of life: Who are we?; Where are we?; What is wrong?; and What is the solution?

5

Sacramentality and Hispanic Popular Religion

The Guadalupe event reveals the sacramental nature of preaching to Latinos.[1] This is the key for entering into the Hispanic imagination. Kevin Irwin seeks to recover a sacramental worldview that sees the world as "a locus where God is revealed, disclosed and experienced."[2] The ramifications of this recovery of sacramentality provide a general framework for celebrating the liturgy and the seven sacraments.[3] Signs and symbols become important in how they are used for worshiping God. They serve as means that transmit meaning and grace. Although sacramentality is true of Catholic worship in any culture and in every time, it is more visibly so in the context of Hispanic ministry in the U.S. in 2022. This heightened sense of sacramentality is one gift among others that Latino Catholics bring to the U.S. Catholic Church.

As a way of introducing a discussion on the Hispanic sacramentality, I would like to share with you a humorous encounter between a Mexican Protestant seminary teacher and his student, Justo Gonzalez:

> When I was growing up [as a Methodist], I was taught to think of such things as the Virgin of Guadalupe as pure superstition. Therefore, I remember how surprised I was at the reaction of a Mexican professor in seminary

---

[1] I will use the phrase "preaching to Latinos" for simplicity to convey the cross-cultural preacher attempting to preach the gospel to the Hispanic culture in the U.S. in 2022. This culture is predominately Mexican-American.

[2] Kevin Irwin, "A Sacramental World—Sacramentality as the Primary Language of the Sacraments," *Worship* 76 (May 2002): 199. See also James Empereur and Eduardo Fernandez, *La Vida Sacra: Contemporary Hispanic Sacramental Theology* (Lanham, Maryland: Rowman & Littlefield Publishers, 2006), 24–31.

[3] Irwin, 199.

when one of my classmates made some disparaging remarks about Guadalupe. The professor, who was as Protestant as they come and who often stooped because he was then elderly, drew himself up, looked at my friend in the eye, and said: "Young man, in this class you are free to say anything you please. You may say anything about me. You certainly are welcome to say anything you wish about the pope and the priests. But don't you touch my little Virgin!"[4]

The Basilica of Our Lady of Guadalupe in Mexico City. *Source:* Photo by Christopher Zaragoza.

4 Roberto Goizueta, *Caminemos con Jesus: Toward a Hispanic/Latino Theology of Accompaniment* (Maryknoll, NY: Orbis Books, 1995), 8.

One important observation from this encounter is that all Latinos, even Protestants, have Catholic roots. Latino culture and Catholicism have deep, historical links. Another is the deep reverence instilled in Hispanic peoples because of their traditions and customs expressed in popular religion. Before delving more deeply into Hispanic sacramentality, I will highlight Hispanic popular religion as the visible expression of the Hispanic worldview.

Statues of indigenous people venerating the image of Mary on the tilma. *Source:* Photo by Christopher Zaragoza.

A major aspect of Hispanic culture is popular religion. As I write this chapter, the vigil of Our Lady of Guadalupe is upon us. Hispanic parishioners will start arriving at the parish on the evening of the December 11th. After purchasing flowers, vases, and candles, they will adorn the shrine set up for the special occasion. The statue of Our Lady of Guadalupe is on the right side of the church and that is where the pilgrims will place their flowers and candles. They will sing *mañanitas* to her at midnight tonight in a Liturgy of the Word led by the deacon. Tomorrow, I will lead *mañanitas* service at 5:30 am and begin a morning Mass afterwards. I love this celebration because it shows the deep devotion of Hispanic parishioners. They kneel before their mother, Our Lady of Guadalupe, asking her to intercede for their families. They pour out their hearts before her. Observing the embodied rituals unveils the sacramental worldview of Latinos. They will visit the church all day on December 12th. At 5:00 pm we will enjoy watching Azteca dancers perform and at 6:00 pm we will listen to a mariachi band serenade Our Lady. We will celebrate a solemn Mass at 7:00 pm and afterward, we will go to the parish hall for a feast.

This celebration of Our Lady of Guadalupe is a highpoint of the Hispanic liturgical year.[5] It is the most well attended liturgical service, far surpassing Christmas and Easter. It is at the heart of the popular religion of Latinos in the U.S. But this celebration leads us to the question of what we are observing: what is popular religion? Pope St. John Paul II noted the influence of popular religion as a resource of the Church of America:

> A distinctive feature of America is an intense popular piety, deeply rooted in the various nations. It is found at all levels and in many sectors of society, and it has special importance as a place of encounter with Christ for all those who in poverty of spirit and humility of heart are sincerely searching for God (cf. Mt 11:25). This piety takes many forms: "Pilgrimages to shrines of Christ, of the Blessed Virgin and the Saints, prayer for the souls in purgatory, the use of sacramentals (water, oil, candles . . .). These and other forms of popular piety are an opportunity for the faithful to encounter the living Christ."[6]

The "popular" part of popular religion means neither "common" nor "well-liked." Rather, it refers to these symbols, narratives, and rituals are *of the people*. Often, the people who adhere to these practices are marginalized.[7]

---

[5] See chapter VIII for an explanation of the Hispanic Liturgical Year and how it differs from the official liturgical year of the Latin Rite in Roman Catholic Church.

[6] John Paul II, *Ecclesia in America*, January 22, 1999, 16. This quote is from *Propositio* 21.

[7] Goizueta, *Caminemos*, 21–22.

Another necessary clarification is the difference between Hispanic popular religion and Euro-American devotional piety. Both are forms of popular Catholicism, but the socio-historical contexts between the two differ. Euro-American devotionalism became widespread especially in the nineteenth century as a way of encouraging identification with the Catholic Church within a hostile Protestant culture. The Catholic hierarchy officially sanctioned this devotion.[8] While the clergy usually led it, it was individual—not communal—in character. Roman Catholic devotions accompanied the liturgy as a supplement or led to the liturgy. Nevertheless, they often displaced liturgy from the center of Catholic life.[9] For example, before Vatican II pious Catholics would often pray the Rosary during the celebration of the Latin Mass.

On the other hand, U.S. Hispanic popular religion emerges in the opposite socio-historical context. Because indigenous people were not supported by the hierarchy, they were often excluded from full participation in official religion. Because their access to the holy through official channels was denied, the poor and marginalized expressed cultural and religious identity in the forms of popular religion.[10] Popular religion combined medieval roots from the Iberian peninsula with indigenous elements. Families, rather than clergy, passed on these traditions and customs. They were more communal activities, which much of the institutional church considered marginal. They represented ways for Latinos to defend themselves from the dominant culture.[11]

Roberto Goizueta draws the attention of Catholic Hispanic theologians to popular religion as an essential element of *locus theologicus*, the place in and from which they do their theological reflection.[12] For U.S. Latinos/as, popular religion represents the Latino community's way of being Catholic. In and through rituals, prayers, processions, devotions, and celebrations, Latinos/as live their Catholic faith.[13]

For Euro-American Catholics the locus of Catholic identity is the parish. "How many people attend Mass on Sundays?" "How many registered parishioners are in the parish?" For Anglos, the answers to these questions determine the strength of a parish. In contrast, the locus for Catholic identity for U.S. Latinos is the home. That is where Latinos practice their Catholic faith.

8 Goizueta, *Caminemos*, 26.
9 Empereur and Fernandez, 24.
10 Goizueta, *Caminemos*, 26.
11 Empereur and Fernandez, 24.
12 Goizueta, *Caminemos*, 19.
13 Roberto Goizueta, *Christ Our Companion: Toward a Theological Aesthetics of Liberation* (Maryknoll, New York: Orbis, 2009), 50.

Las posadas is a ritual reenactment of Mary and Joseph seeking lodging before Jesus is born; it is celebrated right before Christmas. *Source:* Joanie McMahon.

Why did the home became the locus of Catholic identity for Latinos? For centuries Latino/a Catholics have not had access to clergy, except for once every month or two when the circuit-rider priest came into town to baptize, celebrate Mass, hear Confession, and administer other sacraments. That cleric was not likely to be native-born; even today, the vast majority of Catholic priests in most of Latin America are foreigners. Therefore, the home became the center of worship for many people out of necessity. People had to nurture their faith if they were to maintain it and hand it on to the next generation. Thus, popular Catholicism is "of the people" in that its roots are not clerical, but fundamentally lay. The ministers who look after the spiritual well-being of the community are not primarily the priests, but the *abuelitas* (the grandmothers).[14]

What then is the connection between popular religion practiced by the laity mainly in homes and official religion, also known as Christian Tradition? Orlando Espin and Sixto Garcia note the intrinsic connection between what they call "two visions of the Christian Tradition":

> If the contents of the two visions of the Tradition were to be synoptically compared, we would find significant differences in the symbolic, cultural, and analogical use of language, in liturgical expressions and in doctrinal

[14] Goizueta, *Christ Our Companion*, 51.

emphases.... We do not believe, however, that significant differences will be found in the *essential* elements of the faith.... In other words, when careful examination is made of the "official" and "popular" versions of Tradition, the two will be found to be *essentially* the same, though culturally and symbolically expressed in different manners, and with doctrinal and praxical emphases that deeply reveal the socio-historical realities and interests of the holders of either vision of the Tradition. We further believe that it is these socio-historical realities and interests that ultimately create the significant distinctions between these two strands of Christian Tradition.[15]

Another way to approach the relationship between Christian Tradition and popular religion is the process of inculturation. Latinos practice popular religion because the gospel has become inculturated in their context. Spanish missionaries brought the gospel to indigenous peoples, and the mixture or *mestizaje* of these two cultures resulted in the gospel being inculturated in the new world. The descendants of this *mestizaje* (mixture) then emigrated to the U.S., producing yet another *mestizaje* (mixture) or inculturation of the gospel.

Goizueta approaches this issue by talking about the "big Story" and the "little stories." He states: "If the lived faith of the Christian community (what has traditionally been called the *sensus fidelium*) is the key locus of God's revelation in history, the central function of popular Catholicism as an expression of that *sensus fidelium* calls for a reexamination of the relationship between the official tradition and the popular traditions of the church."[16] Goizueta reaffirms Eucharistic worship as essential and central while at the same time resisting the tendency to reduce worship to eucharistic worship alone. Popular religious practices call into question the "eucharization" of the liturgy.[17] In other words, the liturgy of the Church should not be limited to the Eucharist, but should include other forms of worship, such as popular religion.

If popular religious practices are allowed to engage the official liturgical celebrations, both might be enriched in the process. Tradition itself is a product of popular traditions.[18] In other words, the little stories should benefit the Big Story and the Big Story should benefit the little stories. They should be mutually beneficial. What happens when the Big Story neglects

---

15 Sixto Garcia and Orlando Espin, "Lilies of the Field: A Hispanic Theology of Providence and Human Responsibility," *Proceedings of the Catholic Theological Society of America* 44 (1989): 75. See also Goizueta, *Christ Our Companion*, 24.

16 Goizueta, *Christ Our Companion*, 54.

17 Goizueta, *Christ Our Companion*, 55.

18 Goizueta, *Christ Our Companion*, 55.

the little stories? A possible result is that the Big Story will no longer speak to the people. Keith Pecklers argues:

> The Church and its liturgy have no future if they are relegated to a form and structure with a distant and exalted language, removed from ordinary people and ordinary lives. Popular religion offers a great corrective here precisely because it is so accessible to simple and ordinary people and empowers them to recognize their own dignity and role within the wider Church.[19]

Pastoral ministers would be wise to pay attention to the people's practices of popular religion and adapt their preaching, teaching, and pastoral care to the expressions, rituals, and stories revealed in people's practices. If the language of the liturgy is too distant from the people's lived experience, pastoral ministers can attempt to bridge this gap with pastoral charity. Nevertheless, liturgical scholars would be wise to pay attention to the people's common language in preparing liturgical translations that speak to the people.

Offering us a further opportunity to reflect upon Pecklers's advice, Goizueta poses the question of the relationship between official tradition and popular religion. He asks:

> How might the life of the church be enriched if the relationship between the lived faith of the people as embodied in popular Catholicism, or in the *sensus fidelium*, and the official traditions were less unidirectional (traditions → popular traditions) and more truly dialectical (tradition ←→ popular traditions). Indeed, when the Big Story no longer feeds or draws upon the little stories, the Big Story ceases to have any impact on the everyday lives of people; they are no longer willing or able to claim it as their story. When the tradition is uprooted from the popular traditions that nurture it from generation to generation, the tradition will eventually die.[20]

Goizueta is advocating a mutual enrichment between official tradition and popular religious practices. He recommends avoiding both ignoring the role of the popular religious practices in the life of the community and rejecting the central role of Eucharistic worship. Both impoverish the life of faith.

Goizueta holds that only by retrieving the integral relationship between Eucharistic worship and popular religion can we adequately understand each of these dimensions and allow each to find its proper place in the community's liturgical life.[21] He quotes Pecklers for support: "The symbolic

---

[19] Keith Pecklers, *Worship: A Primer in Christian Ritual* (Collegeville: Liturgical Press, 2005), 148.
[20] Goizueta, *Christ Our Companion*, 55–56.
[21] Goizueta, Christ Our Companion, 56.

richness and cultural traditions inherent in popular religiosity can enhance tremendously our liturgical life... and in this way prepare the faithful for a more active liturgical participation. On the other hand, the official liturgy can be instructive for the varied devotions in popular religiosity."[22] Goizueta's project is that the official tradition as expressed in Eucharistic worship and popular religion of the people become mutually enriching. He sees this union of integral worship as the fulfillment of John Paul II's vision of *ecclesia in America*.[23]

Thus far, I have observed the role of popular religion in the life of U.S. Catholic Latinos, attempted to define popular religion, distinguished it from Roman Catholic devotionalism, discussed the importance of the home for Latinos, and argued for a mutual enrichment between official Catholicism and popular religion of Latinos. In the next chapter, I ask the question, "What are the historical roots of popular religion?"

Questions for Reflection and Discussion

1. What is popular religion? What are your observations and experiences of popular religion? How does it differ from popular devotions?

2. Popular religion and official religion represent two strands of the Christian Tradition. What do you think of this assertion?

3. The Big Story and the little stories are another way of talking about the relationship between official religion and popular religion. Do you find this explanation helpful? Why or why not?

4. What might an integral relationship between Eucharistic worship and popular religion look like? What is the relationship between Sunday Eucharist and how you live your faith the other six days of the week?

5. Do you find the Lord in signs, symbols, stories, or someplace else?

---

[22] Goizueta, *Christ Our Companion*, 56.
[23] Goizueta, *Christ Our Companion*, 57.

6

The Historical Roots of Hispanic Popular Religion

In Chapter 1, "One Example from History," I introduced to you Robert de Nobili, a historical example of cross-cultural preaching. He was able to master the culture and language of the people of India and effectively preach the gospel to them. While this perspective is derived from zooming in on one particular person and his ministry from the seventeenth century, I will now attempt to look through a panoramic lens from the discovery of the New World by Christopher Columbus in 1492, and the end of the Council of Trent in 1563. I will begin with a general outline of the *Conquista* (the conquest) before discussing the *Reconquista* (the reconquest) of Spain which preceded it. Next, I will examine the Council of Trent and its influence on Spain and the Americas, especially regarding the practice of popular religion. The chapter will highlight the medieval baroque popular religion that the Franciscans missionaries brought with them to the New World. Entering into this experience of Catholic Tradition points a way to living Catholicism more deeply and as a source of Church renewal and unity.

Twenty-seven years after Columbus's discovery of the New World, Spanish *conquistadores* and Franciscan missionaries began to arrive to set out to conquer this new land. In 1519, Hernan Cortes began the conquest of the Aztecs, the largest indigenous tribe in what today is Mexico. In 1521, Cortes captured the great city of Tenochtitlan, the center of the Aztec empire. In 1523, three Franciscans arrived in Mexico in response to Cortes's request to the king of Spain, Charles V, to send Franciscan friars to begin the process of evangelization. Twelve more Franciscans were sent one year later.[1]

---

1 Eduardo Fernandez, *Mexican-American Catholics* (Mahwah, New Jersey: Paulist Press, 2008), 8–9.

Other key dates include Fray Juan de Zumarraga's appointment as bishop for Mexico City in 1528 and the apparition of Our Lady of Guadalupe to St. Juan Diego on December 12,1531.[2] Recall that Juan Diego brought the message of Our Lady of Guadalupe to Bishop Zumarraga requesting that he build a church in honor of Mary under the title of Our Lady of Guadalupe so that the indigenous people could bring their concerns to her as their spiritual mother. Less than twenty years later, nine million inhabitants had become Christians.

Now for an overview of the state of the culture and society in Spain that influenced the *conquistadores* and the missionaries as they sought to bring the Catholic faith to the New World. For many centuries before 1492, Muslims had occupied Visigothic Spain, which had become a country shaped by Islamic, Christian, and Jewish contributions. This period was not a dark age, but one of cross-cultural flourishing. Gradually, Christianity reasserted itself and pushed out the Islamic rulers in a period called the *Reconquista*.[3] "This period, which concluded with the discovery of the New World and the exploration of men like Christopher Columbus, was a time of light and shadows. Brilliance of learning, the arts, and the commitment to religious values shaped Iberian Catholicism of that time. These were sometimes overshadowed and often mitigated by the accompanying cruelty, militarism, and intolerance."[4]

While Columbus was encountering the New World in 1492, King Fernando and Queen Isabella, having united their kingdoms militarily, now banished Spanish Jews and Muslims or demanded their conversions to unite their kingdom religiously. Taking back from the Muslims what had been originally parts of Christendom was the goal of the *Reconquista*. In addition, the losses that the Roman Church was experiencing in Europe at the time of the Protestant Reformation, made Spain a great defender and promotor of the Catholic faith, even in the New World.[5] The *Reconquista* was the context of how the *conquistadores* and the Franciscan missionaries saw the world and why they sought to conquer and evangelize the New World. One more historical event can help us situate the *Reconquista* and the *Conquista*: the Council of Trent.

The Council of Trent (1545–63) serves as the concluding event of the panoramic photo of this period that begins with the discovery of the New

---

2 Fernandez, 11, 69.

3 James Empereur and Eduardo Fernandez, *La Vida Sacra: Contemporary Hispanic Sacramental Theology* (Lanham, MD: Rowman & Littlefield, 2006), 33.

4 Empereur and Fernandez, 33.

5 Fernandez, *Mexican-American Catholics*, 7–8.

World in 1492. The bishops of the Roman Catholic Church met in Council as a response to the challenge posed by the Protestant reformers. This Council reaffirmed and strengthened the teaching and governance of the Catholic Church, especially in areas highlighted by the reformers. The Council sought to bring uniformity to Catholic practice and extirpate abuses, which were the cause of much scandal prior to the Protestant Reformation. For my purpose, however, I want to examine Trent's effect on popular religion in sixteenth century Spain and the evangelization of the New World.

William Christian holds that interchange between Spain and the New World was common at the time of the Conquest, between the Conquest and Trent, and following the Council of Trent as well. The example he gives is the existence of confraternities and devotion to the Passion and the crucified Christ.[6] "In Spain these confraternities developed throughout the sixteenth century, and in the seventeenth and eighteenth centuries dramatic images of the crucified Christ became enshrined in parish Churches."[7] This fluidity between Spain and the New World seems unaffected by the reforms of the Council of Trent. Christian asserts:

> The aspects usually selected as "pre-Trent" in Latino religiosity are also "post-Trent" and would have been brought to the New World not just in the first wave of conquest and Christianization, but over the following centuries as well. In Spain the main elements of this religiosity were shared by clergy, both secular and religious, and laypersons alike: devotion expressed through images, a landscape regarded as strewn with sacred places, elaborate attention to death and dying, and expressive connection to sacred figures, strong brotherhoods, a theatrical, affective depiction and reenactment of the Passion and the Nativity. Not until the neo-Jansenism of the late eighteenth century would a substantial portion of the Spanish clergy seriously question these elements.[8]

The Council of Trent, therefore, did not stifle popular religion in Spain or even influence Spanish Catholicism until the late eighteenth century—over two hundred years after the Council. This finding will be important below when the Hispanic experience of Catholicism is contrasted with that of the Anglo-American.

---

6 William Christian, "Spain in Latino Religiosity," in *El Cuerpo de Cristo: The Hispanic Presence in the U.S. Catholic Church*, ed. Peter Casarella and Raul Gomez (New York: Crossroads, 1998), 325–30.

7 Christian, 326.

8 Christian, 326–27.

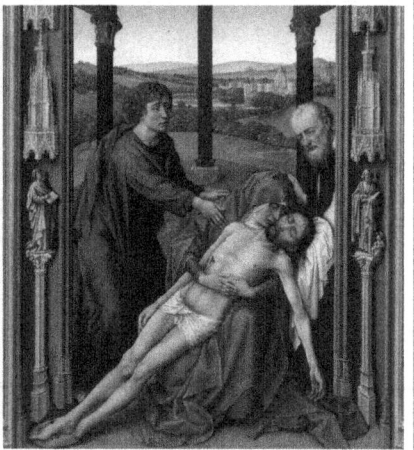

These images depict the worldview of Baroque popular Catholicism from the Iberian peninsula brought to the New World by Spanish missionaries. *Sources:* Top left, Joanie McMahon; Top right, Museu Nacional d'Art de Catalunya, public domain, via Wikimedia Commons; Bottom, © http://www.prestel.com, Prestel Verlag / Rainald Grosshans // Photo: © http://www.bpk-images.de, b p k - Photo Agency / Gemäldegalerie, Staatliche Museen zu Berlin / Jörg P. Anders.

The Catholic experience from the Iberian peninsula was a religious faith rooted in medieval and baroque popular Catholicism. This experience differs greatly from modern Catholicism, especially with respect to different understandings of religious symbols.[9] Medieval Christianity had a unified, profoundly sacramental view of the cosmos. The Creator did not create and withdraw from creation, rather God abided in creation and was encountered

9 Goizueta, *Christ our Companion*, 64.

in it. "All creation was thus assumed to be intrinsically meaningful and intelligible by virtue of the fact that creation was graced from the beginning. The sacred would therefore be encountered, not above or outside creation, but in and through creation."[10]

The religious practices of medieval Christians reflected this organic, sacramental worldview. Goizueta describes their expressions of their faith life: "To them, matter mattered. Religious life was sensually rich; the believer encountered God in the physical environment, through the five senses. The Christian faith of the Middle Ages was firmly anchored in the body: the body of the cosmos, the body of the person, the body of Christ."[11] The mystery of the Incarnation teaches us that "the Word became flesh and dwelt among us, and we have seen his glory" (Jn. 1:14). This mystery undergirds the sacramental life of the Church and extends to popular piety. In a secular society which is indifferent to spiritual realities the Church's profound understanding of sacraments can be dismissed. Attending to Latinos' popular religion can be a source of renewal for retrieving a deeper, more profound sacramental intuition for greater participation and reverence for the sacramental life of the Church.

Thomas O'Meara draws attention to baroque Catholicism embodied in the elaborate religious symbols and dramatic character of communal religious life. He describes this life in the following way:

> There was a universality in which Catholicism experienced God in a vastness, freedom, and goodness flowing through a world of diversity, movement, and order. Christ appeared in a more human way, filled with a personal love, redemptive and empowering.... The Baroque world was also a theater.... Liturgies, operas, frescos, or palatial receptions were theatrical, and Baroque Christianity was filled with visions and ecstasies, with martyrs, missionaries, and stigmatics.... The theater of the Christian life and the kingdom of God moved from the medieval cosmos and the arena of society to the interior of the Baroque church and the life of the soul. In the Baroque, light pours down through clear windows into the church and states that God is not distant nor utterly different from creatures. God is actively present in the Church and in the Christian.[12]

This medieval-baroque worldview permeated the Catholicism of the Iberian peninsula and was the worldview missionaries brought with them to the New World. In their evangelization efforts, they passed on this worldview to their converts, who adopted it along with its attending rituals. This *mestizaje*

---

10 Goizueta, *Christ our Companion*, 65.

11 Goizueta, *Christ our Companion*, 65.

12 Thomas O'Meara, *Theology of Ministry* (Mahwah, NJ: Paulist Press, 1999), 115–16.

(mixture) of two cultures and peoples is at the root of the worldview of religion that developed in the New World. U.S. Latinos are the heirs of this *mestizaje* (mixture).

This new worldview brought to the United States by Hispanic immigrants differs from the Anglo-Catholicism in the United States because they have different historical roots. What scholars call Anglo-Catholicism originates in northern European post-Tridentine Roman Catholicism, whereas the roots of Latin American Catholicism are found in Iberian medieval and baroque Christianity. It was not until the late eighteenth century that medieval worldview was seriously threatened in Spain.[13] "Consequently, Iberian Catholicism was not forced to develop a response to the Reformers' arguments or rebut them point by point—as, also, European Catholics in the United States would later be forced to do."[14]

Because of the Protestant threat to Catholic orthodoxy, northern European Catholicism became increasingly rationalistic, marked by clarity, precision, and uniformity in doctrinal formulations that were not necessary in Spain. The Spanish had just expelled the Jews in 1492 and were in the wake of the *Reconquista*.[15] "It would be the more rationalist, northern European Catholicism that would take hold in the English colonies, an understanding of Catholicism that continues to inform the U.S. Catholic establishment to this day."[16]

Another difference between Latino Catholicism and Anglo-Catholicism is the interaction of the missionaries with the cultures they encountered in the new world. Iberian Catholicism shared a worldview of medieval Catholicism like that of the Amerindian culture. "Conversely, like the English colonizers as a whole, Anglo-American Catholicism generally rejected any such intermingling with the indigenous culture, preferring to expel and exclude rather than subjugate and subdue that culture."[17]

The medieval roots of Latino American popular piety contribute to its noninstitutional character. Popular Catholicism draws from the symbolic, liturgical, and evangelical resources of institutional Catholicism and contributes to the development of broader, official resources. For example, the popularity of the celebration of Our Lady of Guadalupe has grown beyond the borders of Mexican Catholicism.[18] Goizueta does not see this aspect, however, as the source of vitality for popular Catholicism:

---

13 Christian, 326–27.
14 Goizueta, *Christ Our Companion*, 57.
15 Goizueta, *Christ Our Companion*, 65, 57.
16 Goizueta, *Christ Our Companion*, 65, 57.
17 Goizueta, *Christ Our Companion*, 58.
18 Goizueta, *Christ Our Companion*, 60.

> Yet the vitality of popular Catholicism comes primarily from its intimate connection to the everyday life of the people, particularly its deep, intimate connection to domestic life. Likewise, religious leadership is not primarily male and clerical but female and lay; traditions are not passed down primarily through official ecclesiastical organs but through educational and catechetical structures that are quite tangential to the official, sacramental life of the parish.[19]

This is a different vision of the Church. It is noninstitutional and focused on popular religion, with "popular" meaning from the people and their attempts to encounter the divine in *lo cotidiano* (the aspects of daily life).

This vision of the Church reflects the premodern roots of Latino/a popular Catholicism. Goizueta points out that "the exclusive identification of the church with the institution, hierarchy, juridical structure, and clergy only became widespread and entrenched in the wake of the Protestant Reformation, as a defense against the challenges it presented."[20] Avery Dulles distinguishes between the Church as an institution and institutionalism. The Church has always had an institutional element, such as recognized ministers, accepted confessional formulas, and prescribed forms of worship. These elements do not, however, imply institutionalism, which is a system in which the institutional element is primary. Dulles calls institutionalism a deformation of the true nature of the church, which has unfortunately affected the Church at certain points in history.[21] Dulles avers:

> Catholic theology in the Patristic period and in the Middle Ages, down through the great Scholastic doctors of the thirteenth century, was relatively free of institutionalism. The strongly institutionalist development occurred in the late Middle Ages and the Counter Reformation, when theologians and canonists, responding to attacks on the papacy and hierarchy, accented precisely those features that the adversaries were denying. ... The institutional outlook reached its culmination in the second half of the nineteenth century, and was expressed with singular clarity in the first schema of the Dogmatic Constitution on the Church prepared for Vatican Council I.[22]

Although we live in a period of history different from that of Vatican I, perhaps Latino popular piety could help the U.S. Church retrieve a part of

---

19 Goizueta, *Christ Our Companion*, 60.
20 Goizueta, *Christ Our Companion*, 60.
21 Avery Dulles, *Models of the Church* (New York: Doubleday, 1987), 34–35.
22 Dulles, 36.

the tradition when the Church was viewed less as an institution. Perhaps this retrieval could serve as a source of Church renewal.

The effects of the evangelization of the New World are alive and well in the Hispanic experience of popular piety in the United States. Baroque and medieval Catholicism before the Council of Trent were the historical roots of this missionary effort. Goizueta's observations bring together the old and the new:

> The same deep faith in God's nearness reappears in Latino/a popular Catholicism, where dramatic reenactments like the *Via Crucis*, the *Posadas*, or the *Pastorela* serve as constant expressions of God's solidarity. It reappears in the polyphonic ambience of our churches, where angels and demons, saints and penitents, celestial stars and spring flowers are fully incorporated into our lives. Having been brought to Latin American by the Spanish, and having interacted with indigenous religions that often embodied similar beliefs in the nearness of the divine, Latino/a popular Catholicism is the embodied memory, with Jesus Christ at its center, that is at the very heart of the Catholic tradition and that evolved in the Iberian Catholicism of the Middle Ages and the baroque.[23]

Having explored the historical roots of popular religion in Latin America and how it differs from the history of European American Catholicism, I will now move to the heart of popular piety and the purpose of this book: the sacramental character of popular religion and preaching to Latinos.

---

[23] Goizueta, *Christ Our Companion*, 69.

Questions for Reflection and Discussion

1. This chapter has many names and dates. Is there any of this historical information that you see as especially important to highlight? Why?
2. What was the worldview of the *Reconquista* that influenced the *conquistadores* and the Franciscan missionaries as they sought to conquer and evangelize the New World?
3. The religious practices of medieval Christians reflected an organic, sacramental worldview. "To them, matter mattered." Discuss this quotation and how it is relevant to the Hispanic Moment.
4. Discuss the effects of the Council of Trent upon northern European Catholicism and its ongoing influence in Catholicism in the United States.
5. Discuss baroque medieval Catholicism that is at the origin of Hispanic Catholicism. Have you experienced this expression of Catholicism? Do you think that it could serve as a source of renewal in today's Church?

7

Sacramentality and Preaching to Latinos

What is sacramentality? In a broad sense, sacramentality is a worldview that sees the world as a locus where God is revealed, disclosed, and experienced. In a narrower sense, sacramentality provides the general framework for the Church's celebration of the liturgy and the seven sacraments. In the sacramental system, signs contain and transmit meaning and grace. Roberto Goizueta, James Empereur, and Eduardo Fernandez have defined the importance of sacramentality in the Hispanic context, explained how sacramentality works practically, and explored the sacramentality of the most important symbols for Latinos.

Goizueta provides a definition of Hispanic sacramentality, by drawing attention to "the fundamentally sacramental character of the U.S. Hispanic way of life, wherein physical existence is seen as intrinsically related to the supernatural, transcendent realm of the sacred."[1] Latinos express this attention to the divine in physical existence through popular religious symbols. Goizueta explains that

> A popular religious symbol is an object, image, or action that reveals, mediates, and makes present what may be called the ineffable, the holy, the sacred, or the supernatural.... Symbols make present here and now what they re-present. Though the ultimate referent of the symbol is beyond itself (e.g., God), the symbol draws us to itself so that we may first encounter this "beyond" *within* the symbol itself. The symbol thus effects a *relationship*

---

[1] Goizueta, *Caminemos*, 19.

between its transcendent, ultimate referent and ourselves—and *among* all of us who together participate in and share that relationship.²

The focal point for the celebration of Our Lady of Guadalupe is the image of Mary imprinted on the *tilma* (cloak) of Juan Diego. When Latinos approach this symbol, they do not make a distinction between the symbol and its ultimate referent beyond itself. When they present flowers and song to the image, they are offering them to Mary herself, their spiritual mother. Although they do not consciously reflect upon this dynamism, the symbol of Our Lady of Guadalupe effects a relationship between Mary and the devotee and among all devotees of Mary in community. The symbol of Mary thus creates relationships.

"She came up behind him and touched the fringe of his cloak, and immediately her flow of blood stopped" (Luke 8:44). *Source:* Joanie McMahon.

Mary and Jesus are the two religious figures or symbols that play especially key roles in popular Catholicism among Latinos. They are prevalent in every aspect of Hispanic life from explicit religious rituals to sayings or *dichos* of everyday life.³ Goizueta holds that "one might even go so far as to say that, for many Latinas and Latinos, religious faith is virtually indistinguishable from our everyday relationship with Jesus and Mary, lived out in everything from the most highly 'institutional' liturgical services to the most intimate, personal devotions—and every aspect of life in between."⁴ Goizueta then asks: If Jesus and Mary are the two central symbols for Latinos, which Jesuses and Marys do they identify with? That is, they do not relate to the figure of Jesus in the abstract, but rather as *el niño Jesús* (the child Jesus), *Jesús, hijo de María* (Jesus, son of Mary), *or Jesús, mi hermano* (Jesus, my brother), or *Cristo, nuestro rey* (Christ, our king). Nevertheless, among all these Jesuses, the one that stands out both in its pervasiveness and centrality is the crucified Lord. The highpoint of the Triduum celebration for Latinos is Good Friday with the focus on the crucified Jesus.⁵

---

2 Goizueta, *Caminemos*, 27.
3 Goizueta, *Caminemos*, 29–30.
4 Goizueta, *Caminemos*, 30.
5 Goizueta, *Caminemos*, 32.

The Mary Latinos identify with is never Mary alone, but always Mary in relationship with her son Jesus. She is always the mother of Jesus for Latinos. She is the *madre dolorosa* (the sorrowful mother), who accompanies Jesus in his passion.[6]

Latinos express their devotion to Mary by honoring her as Our Lady of Guadalupe. Although this reverence is practiced by Mexican Americans, U.S. Latinos from other Latin American countries have also begun to develop a devotion to Our Lady of Guadalupe.[7] In this apparition in Mexico, the bishop initially rejects Juan Diego's message. Only after Juan Diego brings him a sign does he agree to the Virgin's request. The sign was both the roses gathered in his *tilma* and the image of Our Lady of Guadalupe imprinted on Juan Diego's *tilma*. The latter was a miraculous image as a divine object.[8]

The image of Our Lady of Guadalupe reveals many wonders in symbols of new life and beginning. For example, she is pictured as pregnant and wearing a maternity band around her waist. The most obvious symbol is the Lady's olive skin which tells the indigenous people of Mexico that she is one with them.[9] For this reason, she is called *La Morenita* (the little brown skinned one). Both Mary's appearance of the image on the *tilma* and her choice of Juan Diego, a poor, indigenous man, shows Our Lady of Guadalupe's solidarity with the poor and marginalized. Mary's identification with the poor is another reason why Latinos can readily seek her help in new land.

A painting of Our Lady of Guadalupe and a crucifix both are common in the homes of Latinos. These symbols are concrete, palpable, material, and particular, and yet they reveal the universal. The particular symbol of Jesus crucified reveals and manifests the transcendent and divine Jesus, the Son of God and Savior. The particular reveals the universal. Mary is present in the image of Our Lady of Guadalupe and thus reveals herself as universal mother to the person praying in front of the image.

The particular reveals the universal. This observation leads Goizueta to conclude that for Latinos the person is sacrament.[10] That is to say, each person represents and reveals a whole web of relationships: mother, father, cousin, grandfather, nephew, niece, etc. There is no individual without the family and this web of relationships., Unlike Anglo-Americans who talk about work and profession, when Latinos meet someone for the first time, they ask about the person's family: "Who is your father, mother? Where do

---

6 Goizueta, *Caminemos*, 38.

7 Goizueta, *Caminemos*, 38.

8 Goizueta, *Caminemos*, 43.

9 Goizueta, *Caminemos*, 45.

10 Goizueta, *Caminemos*, 48.

you come from? Do I know one of your relatives?" This sacramental understanding of the human person undergirds the Hispanic worldview.

Thus far, I have defined sacramentality for Latinos, talked about how sacramentality works practically, located it in the two major symbols of Jesus and Mary, and explored the person as sacrament. All this has served as helpful background material for the major purpose of this handbook: namely, preaching to Latinos. My hope is that in coming to a greater understanding of Hispanic culture, you would be more effective in preaching to Latinos.

Ideally, preaching to Latinos expresses sacramentality in at least six ways. The first way recognizes that Hispanic culture is visual. Mexico was evangelized by means of an image that portrayed the gospel to the indigenous culture. The missionaries in Mexico added to and built upon the success of evangelization and catechesis brought about by the image of our Lady of Guadalupe. In 1523 Friar Pedro de Gante, an early Franciscan missionary, developed visual equivalents for each phrase or idea represented in the Our Father, the Creed, and the Hail Mary. This successful mode of communication was later extended to preaching by Friar Jacobo de Testera. Seeing the need to preach in pictures sometime around 1529, he used a series of rolled animal hides on which various images could be quickly painted.[11] Today the wise cross-cultural preacher will continue to evangelize and catechize by

Ideographic catechism of Friar Pedro de Gante. Mexico, circa 1525. *Source:* Pedro de Gante (1486–1572), public domain.

---

11 Jaime Lara, "Visual Preaching: The Witness of our Latin Eyes," in *PCLC*, 82.

means of pictures and images. Stained glass windows, icons, statues, candles, crucifixes, Stations of the Cross, the Advent wreath, and religious images serve as symbols that convey the divine to the Hispanic imagination. Flowers and candles are especially powerful.

I have preached visually to Hispanic communities for twenty-three years. In one my first assignments, I celebrated Mass in Spanish for the Solemnity of the Most Holy Trinity. I reinterpreted a replica of the Rublev icon on the Holy Trinity to preach this mystery. Jesus Christ is the central

An example of a preaching aid from Friar Diego de Valdés, Rhetorica Christiana, Perugia, 1579. *Source:* Diego Valadés, "Friar Preaching to Native Converts," 1579, copperplate engraving, within Rhetorica Christiana ad concionandi et orandi usum accommodate [...] ex Indorum maximè deprompta sunt historiis. Perugia: Petrus Jacobus Petrutius, 1579 (Getty Research Institute).

figure dressed in red and blue, the colors of blood and water. After his death, a Roman soldier pierced Jesus with a lance and out of his side flowed blood and water (Jn 19:34). The Fathers of the Church viewed this event as the birth of the Church coming from Jesus side. The water symbolizes Baptism, and the blood symbolizes the Eucharist, the two foundational sacraments of the Church. Jesus' Passion and Death on a cross is symbolized by the tree behind him.

Jesus is not the only person directing his glance to the person of God the Father on the left, but the figure on the right also gazes at God the Father, the creator of heaven and earth. The person of the Holy Spirit leads worshippers to adore God the Father. This mysterious person on the right is clad in green

Source: Andrei Rublev, public domain.

and blue garments. These are the colors of new life: in spring green plants teeming with life grow and flowers blossom. Only with water, however, can living plants grow and flourish. Water is a polyvalent symbol of the Holy Spirit, the Lord and the giver of life.

The person of God the Father wears translucent colored garments as if the mystery of God the Father is beyond our comprehension. Behind him is a building with many rooms, recalling the gospel in which Jesus says, "In my Father's house there are many rooms" (Jn. 14:2).

One last point is that Jesus' hand stretches out to the chalice of the Eucharist, which contains his blood. The three persons of the Trinity are seated around a table. The Father and the Holy Spirit have a space between them for us. We are invited to the eucharistic banquet when we gather to celebrate the Mass. We enter into the mystery of the Father, the Son, and the Holy Spirit.

In another church for a different assignment, I preached the paschal mystery to Latinos with the help of the stained-glass windows. The congregation, of course, immediately recognized Jesus' Passion and Death and found his Resurrection quite easily. Jesus emerges triumphantly from the tomb; two Roman soldiers faint because of fright at this event. The mystery of Pentecost is also apparent. Tongues of fire descend from heaven and come to rest on the disciples and the woman dressed in blue, the Virgin Mary, who accompanies the disciples in prayer waiting for the outpouring of the Holy Spirit from heaven. What is not readily apparent is the mystery of the Ascension. Nevertheless, if one looks closely, one can see it. Between the mystery of the Resurrection and Pentecost a small white cloud with a cross is evident. The designer of these stained-glass windows wants us to see the Ascension as the linking of the mysteries of the Resurrection and Pentecost. The cloud recalls Luke's account of Jesus' returning to heaven: "As they [the disciples] were looking on, he [Jesus] was lifted up, and a cloud took him out of their sight" (Acts 1:9).

The second way preaching to Latinos expresses sacramentality is the oral nature of Hispanic communication. Many Latinos struggle to read or write in Spanish and in English. Although writing a column in the bulletin in English is an effective way to communicate to Anglo parishioners, it is largely an ineffective way to communicate to the Latinos because, even if they can read it, which many cannot, they do not end up reading the bulletin. They do pay close attention, however, to the announcements after Mass. The cross-cultural preacher will attend to the oral aspects of good communication: tone, pitch, enthusiasm, lowering and raising one's voice, etc. Studying narrative and storytelling in Latino culture would be a further way to enhance cross-cultural preaching.

Attending to these aspects of the oral nature of Hispanic communication, I have learned by trial and error that the best way to preach is without notes and manuscript. The message needs to be interiorized earlier in the week. Reading the homily is a recipe for disaster because it will bore the Hispanic audience. Preachers need to have a heart-to-heart conversation with Latinos in a way that they can understand. Be simple without being simplistic. That is, preach with depth regarding the mysteries of God and the human condition, but in uncomplicated language. Preachers should follow the adage "show me; don't tell me." After clearly stating the one central theme, homilists should develop their message with stories, anecdotes, *dichos* (aphorisms), examples, and illustrations. Preachers need to paint a picture Latinos can "see" with the mind's eye.

Dichos are aphorisms that reveal the wisdom of Hispanic culture. Preachers can study these, memorize them, and employ them when preaching. Some examples include *Panza llena corazón contento* (full stomach makes a happy heart), *ojos vemos corazones no sabemos* (appearances can be deceiving), and *Dios aprieta pero no ahorca* (God squeezes but does not strangle). It is not uncommon for Latinos in the U.S. to come from rural areas in their countries of origin. The *dichos* reflect this rural, simple culture in which wisdom is passed from generation to generations by short, pithy sayings. Latinos love to hear *dichos* and will listen and respond enthusiastically when preachers preach in "their language."

The third way preaching to Latinos expresses sacramentality is to recognize that Hispanic culture is a high-context/low-content culture. "That is to say that what is said (content) is often secondary in importance to how something is said (context)."[12] Here the cross-cultural preacher must go forward with fear and trembling. The Euro-American way is to get to the point and be direct, especially in dealing with conflict. The Hispanic way is to eventually arrive at the problem, but in a circuitous manner that shows that one values the relationship. This idea is foreign cross-cultural preachers, and most would benefit from seeking advice and input from Latinos as to how to say something difficult in way that shows the relationship is valued.

After twenty-three years of Hispanic ministry, I often reflect upon what has worked well and what has not worked. I think one area that has not worked well was having to explain difficult matters to people. I think I was perhaps too blunt, lacking compassion and concern. This is difficult for the Anglo pastor with a large Latino community, especially if he wants to provide good, courageous, bold leadership by articulating a vision. My vision was

---

[12] Jorge Presmanes, "The Juxtaposition of Dangerous Memories: Toward a Latino Theology of Preaching from the Underside of the Diaspora Experience," in *PCLC*, 22–23.

faith-formation at all levels for all parishioners. Some neighboring parishes required one year of faith formation before receiving the sacraments of first Communion and Confirmation. Our parish required four as a minimum. Ideally, we wanted children to have faith formation at every grade level from kindergarten to senior year of high school. In setting forth these requirements, I made statements like, "This is our parish and the way we do things; if you don't like it, you are free to go to a different parish." While this was true, I question whether I should have said it. I do not think I prepared the Latinos to hear this. I think I could have had more pastoral wisdom and charity when explaining difficult policies.

The fourth way preaching to Latinos expresses sacramentality relates to the third way of a high-context/low-content culture: relationships matter! I was at a preaching conference at Notre Dame in 2014 just as I was beginning my new pastorate in a shared parish with a large Latino population. During one of the breaks, I had the fortune of meeting Gustavo Gutierrez, the famous liberation theology theologian. I asked him what one piece of advice he would give me as I began a new pastorate among Latinos. He replied, "*Amistad*." This word *amistad* is the Spanish word for friendship. Good cross-cultural preaching will demonstrate how important family relationships and friendships are and also the role and importance of *padrinos* (the godparents) in the family.[13] The sacramental character of family relationships is another effective way of preaching to Latinos.

I was fortunate enough to have weekend help from a priest who loved Hispanic ministry. He embodied this relationship principle of preaching to Latinos by remembering names. Every time he would meet someone, he would write their name down on a 3x5 card which he carried in his shirt pocket. He would later review that list and often pray for specific needs mentioned in the course of conversation. One of the sweetest words we hear in our native tongue is someone saying our name. This priest understood this. Remembering someone's name improves our relationships with them.

How does remembering names help with preaching to Latinos? I encourage you to make your preaching to Latinos conversational. Ask questions and call on people by name. Preach as if you are having a one-on-one conversation with one of your Hispanic parishioners. Knowing people's names and voicing them in the homily helps make preaching a dialogue between the preacher and the people. In this dialogue, show people love, mercy, and hope. Help them to know that Jesus loves them and wants them to grow close to

---

13 Nicole Flores, "Latina/o Families: Solidarity and the Common Good," *Journal of the Society of Christian Ethics* 33, no. 2 (2013): 61. Accessed Nov. 28, 2016. ATLASerials, Religion Collection, EBSCOhost.

him. Like the Virgin Mary, Jesus wants to shepherd them, guide them, and help them with their problems. Latinos should come away from the homily saying, "Father knows my name and he cares about me and my family. He loves me and he tells me that I am loved and accepted by God."

The fifth way of preaching to Latinos that expresses sacramentality is testimony. Preaching as testimony is powerful for Latinos because preachers talk about what they have seen and heard.[14] They talk about God at work in the world today. Preachers say, "God did this for me, and he can do this also for you." Latinos have a great deal of faith and want to see God's action in their lives and the lives of others. Good cross-cultural preachers will rely upon giving testimonies as a way of effectively conveying the gospel.

For the eleventh Sunday in Ordinary Time Year B, I preached to a Hispanic congregation on the parable of the mustard seed from Mark's Gospel (Mark 4:30-32). Jesus tells this parable to provide a picture of his ministry. Jesus plants the mustard seed in the most unlikely of places, and this smallest of all seeds becomes a large bush with many boughs providing shade for people and allowing birds to nest in its branches. In his encounter with the Samaritan woman in John 4, Jesus plants the small seed of the gospel in her heart. This seed takes root and produces fruit: she accepts Jesus and his message, and she goes and tells the Samaritans from her hometown that Jesus is the Messiah. They come and hear him and then come to believe in him. The small seed Jesus plants in this Samaritan woman produces an abundant harvest (Jn 4:4-42).

I provided two testimonies to illustrate how the seed of God's Word, although small, can surprise us by its abundant growth. George is a math teacher at a local high school. At graduation time, students often return from college and visit their teachers. One student had a conversation with George and thanked him for teaching him mathematics and also for something he had said that led to a change in in this young man's life. Upon further reflection, George could not remember what he said to this young man that later produced such a transformation. George reminded himself of the parable of the mustard seed. In his routine of teaching and administration, he was daily scattering small seeds in the hearts of his students not knowing what would produce fruit. One seed found rich soil and with the help of God's grace led to an abundant harvest in the life of this college student even though George couldn't recall it.

Pablo (Paul) served as the coordinator of Hispanic ministry in the parish. His vision for the transformation of the Latino community was to train

---

[14] Justo Gonzalez and Pablo Jiménez, *Púlpito: An Introduction to Hispanic Preaching* (Nashville: Abingdon Press, 2005), 63; See also Anna Carter Florence's *Preaching as Testimony* (Louisville: Westminster John Knox Press, 2007).

leaders who would then be able to lead various ministries in the parish. With this goal in mind, Pablo invited Hispanic volunteers to receive training from the archdiocese's Latino Ministry office. The office sponsors four *institutos* (institutes or classes) for Hispanic formation, including catechesis, bible, leadership, and theology. Various priests would serve as teachers in these institutes. The Latinos in the parish accepted Pablo's invitations and met on Saturdays from September through May. One year forty-three parishioners graduated, the highest total of any of the parishes in the archdiocese. A good number of these trained leaders served as catechists. The small seed Pablo planted flourished not only in these forty-three people, but also in the many children they taught. One year Pablo had enrolled over two hundred fifty children in faith formation! Pablo's small seeds planted in Latino volunteers led to a great harvest.

The sixth way is preaching as performance.[15] The missionaries in Mexico employed the dramatic arts to evangelize and catechize. This manner of preaching and teaching involved depictions of the Last Judgment and scenes from the life of Christ. By capturing their imaginations, these productions had a dramatic effect upon the indigenous people. This entertainment was instructive and served the purpose of handing on the faith.[16]

One Hispanic seminarian preached to the class on the occasion of a baptism. He acted out the baptism and painted a picture of the *padrinos* (godparents) and *padres* (parents) bringing their children to the font for Baptism. It's as if he was painting the picture for us so that we could see in our mind's eye what was happening. This was preaching in Spanish but in a way that the congregation could understand because the seminarian acted out the scene. Some of the students understood Spanish well, some a little, and others not at all. Nevertheless, all were able to get something out of the homily because the seminarian preached as if it were a performance.

There are similarities between African-American or Black preaching and preaching to Latinos. When I preach cross-culturally to Latinos, I often employs call and response, and the congregation enjoys the interaction. Pope Francis also preaches this way. Call and response is embodied preaching. Latinos listen with their ears, and they respond with their voices or by raising their hands. Preaching to Latinos needs to be embodied to reach the hearts of the people. One approach I used when preaching about Moses raising his hands above his head as he prayed the Israelites on to victory over Amalek (Exodus 17:8–13) was to encourage the people to raise their hands. I preached

---

15 See Jana Childers and Clayton Schmit's *Performance in Preaching: Bringing the Sermon to Life* (Grand Rapids: Baker Academic, 2008).

16 Lara, 85–86.

about the *orans* (praying) position of prayer and encouraged them to pray with their hands held above their head both during the Our Father at Mass and at home in personal prayer. I have found that if I model what I preach with my body, then the people follow by doing what I do. Preaching to Latinos needs to be embodied to be effective.

In summary, the key concept to preach effectively to Latinos is to demonstrate sacramentality as it manifests itself in the two most important persons of Jesus and Mary. This background provided the foundation to explore the six ways that effective preaching to Latinos expresses a deep sacramentality. But preaching the gospel to Latinos effectively requires an understanding of how sacramentality expresses itself in the sacramental rituals of the Church. To this endeavor I now turn.

Questions for Reflection and Discussion

1. What is sacramentality, and how is it revealed in Hispanic culture and in the liturgy?
2. What does it mean to say that "the person is sacrament"? Why is this statement important for our understanding and life in the Church?
3. Preaching to Latinos is ideally both visual and oral. What are the benefits of focusing on these two aspects of preaching to Latinos?
4. What is a high-context/low-content culture? Do you have any experience of this type of culture? Please elaborate.
5. Preaching to Latinos ideally involves testimony and performance. What is your experience of this kind of preaching?

Hispanic Sacramentality and the Sacraments in Youth

Before I begin to trace the Hispanic Sacramentality through the life of a Latino person, I want to introduce the distinction between the insider and outsider researcher. Insiders are those individuals whose personally relevant social world is under study, whereas outsiders are seeking knowledge for its own sake.[1] In this preaching manual, Hispanic parishioners are insiders whose religious practices I am examining. I am the outsider in that I am not Hispanic, but a Caucasian of European-American roots and not a native speaker of the Spanish language. My education, training in theology, and status as a priest also contribute to my perspective as an outsider. In addition, many of the scholars I cite are outsiders. Nevertheless, because I serve as pastor of the parish, I am also an insider. I have a vested interest in the success of my parish that prevents me from being a dispassionate, neutral third party. Rather than seeing my position as an insider-outsider as untenable, I see it as an advantage. Brett Hoover gives a few reasons why:

> Both the outsider and the insider have a privileged epistemological perspective—the outsider on account of formal training, a discipline of detachment, and the desire for generalizable results, the insider on account of membership in the studied community and concern with particular results and their practical application. Put another way, we might say that one privileges experience-distant concepts and the other experience-near concepts. Combining these perspectives creates a new and marginal

---

[1] Brett Hoover, *The Shared Parish: Latinos, Anglos, and the Future of U.S. Catholicism* (New York: New York University Press, 2014), 227.

perspective with all its attendant creative tensions. New questions and answers surface previously unimagined by outsider or insider alone.[2]

Recognizing the benefits of my insider-outsider position, I will begin my reflections on sacramentality in the life of Latinos over the span of their lifetimes.

The scene is common in the Catholic shared parish with a large Hispanic population. The Mass ends, the priest and the altar servers process to the entrance of the church, the priest puts the *Flor y Canto* hymnal in one of the back pews, and then stands in front of the exit doors to shake parishioners' hands. The large crowd makes it nearly impossible to shake everyone's hand, but that's what Latinos expect. It is considered polite and respectful to greet the priest properly by extending the right hand and shaking it firmly. I often confuse people because I shake with both hands so as to greet as many people as possible. Suspending this custom during the pandemic has disrupted the dynamic of interaction with Latino Catholics.

Often parishioners will ask for a special blessing from the priest—this requires patience from the priest because he has just given everybody in the church a blessing! Nevertheless, Latinos will regularly request a special blessing: *Padre, dame tu bendición* (Father, give me your blessing). *Padre, dale tu bendición a nuestra familia* (Father, give our family a blessing). I want to highlight one particular request for blessing. Often a couple and their children will ask me to bless a child in the womb. I extend my hands and pray for God's blessing for the unborn child in the womb, for protection for the mother, and for blessings upon both parents and their children. Blessing a pregnant woman is a sacramental sign. It shows Christ's love for life and extends this love in the ministry of the Church. For Latinos, sacramentality is evident at the beginning of life—even while they are in the womb.

With big smiles on their faces, Latinos will bring their newborn babies to church and show them to the priest after Mass, again requesting a blessing for their *niño* (child). I usually ask them when they are planning to have the child baptized. "What do I need to do for Baptism?" is a common question. I encourage them to go to the office during the week with the birth certificate, names of the godparents, and a date picked out for Baptism. The day is festive. Our parish customarily celebrates baptisms in groups every second Saturday of the month at 11:00 am. The deacon and I rotate in the role of presider (he does it one month; I do it the next).

Preaching at Baptisms differs from the Sunday homily because it is catechetical in nature. I usually seize the opportunity to provide some basic

---

[2] Hoover, 229–30.

THE SACRAMENTS IN YOUTH

Source: Joanie McMahon.

catechesis by asking two questions. First, why does the Church baptize infants? Second, what does it mean to educate your child in the Catholic faith? Asking these two questions gives the parents, godparents, and guests the opportunity to catechize one another. Common answers to the first question include to be cleansed of original sin, to experience salvation from sin, to become a son or daughter of God, to enter into the life of the church, to receive the Holy Spirit, to become a Catholic.

One answer I highlight is that the Church baptizes infants because she believes Baptism is necessary for salvation, and she wants salvation for these children. Baptists and Evangelical Protestants confuse Latinos by saying that baptism of infants should be postponed until the child reaches maturity and can make a conscious act of faith in Jesus Christ. I remind the listeners that while these children cannot make an adult act of faith, their parents and godparents can make that act for them. I also emphasize that good parents regularly make decisions for the benefit of their children, including friends, schools, entertainment, and more. I tell parents it is a good decision to baptize your children in infancy because you do not want the child to die without having received the grace of Baptism. If a child, however, does die before Baptism, the Church commends them to the mercy of God. She believes in God's mercy and this mercy extends to the unbaptized child. Still, parents should be responsible and seek eternal life for their children by having them baptized.

What does it mean to educate your children in the Catholic faith? Common answers to this question include teaching children the Our Father, the Hail Mary, and the Glory Be, praying at night before bed, teaching them to bless themselves (*persignarse*), inculcating the Ten Commandments by word and example, bringing them to the Eucharist on Sundays and Holy Days, preparing them to receive the sacraments of first Reconciliation, first Communion, and Confirmation, supporting the Church financially, and becoming disciples of the Lord.

Even Latinos who do not participate in the life of the parish by attending Sunday Mass bring their children to the Church for Baptism. Perhaps the reason for this attraction to this sacrament is its deep symbolic character in that it speaks to the Hispanic mindset by appealing to Hispanic sacramentality. The white baptismal garment is an outward symbol of the inner workings of sanctifying grace. The water too symbolizes the death to sin and the birth to a new life in Christ and the Holy Spirit. The anointing with sacred chrism connotes being filled with the Holy Spirit and empowered for mission like Christ. Parents usually designate a *padrino* (a godfather) to approach the Easter candle to light their individual baptismal candle. The presider says, "Receive the light of Christ." When all the families have lighted their baptismal candles, I encourage parents and godparents to grasp the candle together as a new community and to respond enthusiastically to the prayer in the rite which entrusts them with the light of Christ to be kept burning brightly until eternal life. The sacraments create the life of sanctifying grace not only in the lives of those receiving the sacraments; they also create community as new relationships are forged. The cross-cultural preacher will highlight this symbol of the baptismal rite.

This moment in the rite illustrates the Hispanic cultural practice of *compadrazgo* (the institution of godparents). Unlike in Euro-American Catholic communities, the role of godparents carries more responsibility for Latinos. It goes beyond a formality. Parents choose their *padrinos* (godfathers) and *madrinas* (godmothers) carefully because it is a lifetime commitment, often involving significant time and financial resources. The godparents will be present not only at the Baptism, but at first Communion, Confirmation, weddings, and other significant events, such as birthdays, especially *quinceañera* for girls, and graduations. Godparents are expected to contribute financially to these events as well. Godparents become an extension of *la familia* (the family) for Latinos. They often call godparents *compadre* (co-father) or *comadre* (co-mother). Sacraments create community and this visible institution of *compadrazgo* is evident at every Hispanic Baptism.

I would be remiss if I did not mention the baptismal party on the day of a child's baptism. Usually it occurs in a backyard if the weather is nice. The family will invite other family members and close friends. Latinos love to celebrate, and the occasion of a baptism is a wonderful opportunity to be festive. Beer, wine, pop, *carnitas* (pork), beans, rice, and tortillas are omnipresent. And we cannot forget the *pastel* (the cake). Goizueta has written eloquently on Latinos love for *fiesta* (party), entitling his article "Fiesta: Life in the Subjunctive."[3] If the Kingdom of God were here in its fullness, it would be a celebration. Latinos celebrate because the Kingdom of God is here in its infancy, and so we must celebrate, even if the Kingdom has not arrived in its entirety.

The *presentación* (the presentation) of the child is the next milestone. This is a Mexican custom in which the parents bring the child to the Mass and present him or her to the community. This is a minor rite, usually at the end of the Mass. This practice is a way of extending baptism and providing pastoral care for a young child in between Baptism and first Communion. The presentation is not universally practiced by all Hispanic groups. Even in Mexico the practice differs from region to region and is becoming

---

3   Roberto Goizueta, "Fiesta: Life in the Subjunctive," in *From the Heart of our People*, ed. Orlando Espin and Miguel Diaz (Maryknoll, NY: Orbis Books, 1999), 84–99.

increasingly rare. However, the presentation is found more abundantly among young adult immigrants.[4]

In the traditional Mexican custom, the parents make the presentation soon after baptism, that is, within forty days after birth, or alternatively, when the child reaches the age of three. In the first case, the purpose is to invoke divine protection upon the newborn and gratitude for a safe childbirth.[5] In the second case, the parents bring the child to the church and the priest says, "We come to present N. to our Lord and Master. We want our Lord to bless and accept this child as he did those children of his own time. We want this so that this child will be a good Christian in this life and from this moment fulfill his (her) principal purpose here which is to glorify God and so achieve his (her) happiness."[6]

In both cases in my experience, the priest invites the couple to come forward after the Post-Communion Prayer with their newborn or three-year-old, often dressed up. Usually, the parents and siblings are behind the child. The parents will have the newborn in their arms. If the child is a three-year-old, I will have the father or mother lift the child so that the audience can see him or her. The priest extends his hands and then imparts a blessing upon the child. Then the priest invites all the parishioners to give the family a round of applause. This custom recalls the piety of Anne and Joachim, who, according to tradition, brought the Virgin Mary to the Temple for a special blessing when she turned three years old. Latinos wish to continue this custom that they learned from their parents and country of origin.

First Reconciliation and first Communion are the next two sacraments. Our parish's practice is to require a two-year preparation period for both the children and their parents. We call this commitment *catechesis familiar* (family catechesis), and we have experienced much fruit from this approach. Parents meet in the parish hall at 9:00 on Sundays, while their children attend a class in the school. The classes conclude at 10:45, and parents join their children for the Sunday 11:00 am Mass. Because we have so many parents and children, we have a second class that meets in the same format at 11:00 am and concludes at 12:45 pm. Again, parents and their children join together to attend Mass at 1 pm. From the pastor's perspective, I see the benefits of faith formation using the approach of *catechesis familiar*. The parents accompany their children in the learning the Catholic faith, and it is not something in which the parents can take a passive role and merely drop the children off for class. I have taught the parents and have been impressed at their desire to learn more about the things

---

4 Empereur and Fernandez, 79.

5 Empereur and Fernandez, 79.

6 Empereur and Fernandez, 79.

of God. An important added benefit is that this approach fills the church up for two Masses. When we do not have faith formation because of a vacation, Mass attendance drops (and so does the collection).

My observation is that Hispanic parents also place a priority on having their children attend first Communion classes and receiving their first Holy Communion. Perhaps again the reason for this is the deep meaning of Eucharist which appeals to Hispanic sacramentality. The wine and the bread are rich symbols that speak to our need for food and nourishment, the need to feast and to celebrate, the blessings of nature and creation, and the industry of human work. The Eucharist is a memorial of Christ's sacrifice on Calvary and Christ makes himself fully present as the bread and wine are transformed into his Body and Blood. The ritual symbols of the first Communion include a white dress for a young girl or a white suit for a young boy. These clothes highlight the specialness of the celebration and recall the white baptismal garment received at baptism. The godparents accompany the parents on this festive day. They often purchase the religious items the first Communicant carries, such as a Bible and a rosary. A party at home follows the liturgical rite at church. Like for the baptism, Latinos invite friends and family to rejoice on this occasion.

How should a priest, deacon, or bishop preach to Latinos at a first Communion? On most occasions, the gospels are either the Bread of Life discourse from chapter six of John's Gospel or the institution narratives from the synoptic Gospels. I try to keep the message as simple as possible by having a dialogue with the children about the Last Supper, first Communion, and the fruits of the Eucharist. Similar to baptismal preaching, this homily is more catechetical in nature. What did Jesus do on the night before he died? He ate and drank at the Last Supper with his disciples. At the end of the meal, he took bread, blessed it, broke it, gave it to his disciples and said, "Take this and eat it. This is my body which will be given up for you." Then he took a chalice filled with wine and said, "Take this and drink from it. This is the chalice of my blood, the blood of the new and eternal covenant, which will be poured out for you for the forgiveness of sins. Do this in memory of me." I usually ask them, "What was going to happen to Jesus on the next day after the Last Supper?" Then I point to the large crucifix and say, "Jesus was going to die for us so that we could have our sins forgiven."

The next question is, "What happens at your first Communion?" The children respond: "You receive Christ's body to eat and his blood to drink" or "Jesus comes and lives in your heart." Then I add: "This is called the Eucharist. Every time we gather on Sunday, Catholics celebrate the Eucharist. This is your first time to participate fully in this celebration."

Then I ask them "How should you act differently after having received the Eucharist? How should you act at home?" They reply often with look of guilt on their faces: "Obey your mom and dad, do the dishes, clean your room, get along with your brothers and sisters, and only watch good things on TV and the cellphone—not junk." Then I query them about how they should behave in school. They respond: "Obey your teachers, do your homework, be nice, and don't gossip or swear." The homily is a dialogue. They learn about the moral life from the priest and from one another. Catechetical preaching for a first Communion typically involves a moral component and the children tend to understand the new life they are now called to live.

Children also make their first Reconciliation in preparation for first Communion. This is also a moment to confess their sins for the first time to a priest and to receive absolution. Confession is still practiced in the Hispanic community. Whole families will come to confession on the same day, often confessing their sins as well as those of other family members. Children's first Reconciliation initiates them into the family practice of confession. This sacrament also appeals to the Hispanic sensibility because the priest represents Christ, and one confesses one's sins to Christ and receives forgiveness and absolution from him. Latinos seem to understand the importance of going to Confession, taking stock of one's life, and repenting of sin. They know they need the Lord's grace in the struggle against sin.

How should one preach to Latinos at a first Reconciliation? I visited a parish with a large Hispanic community to help the pastor with confessions for children preparing for first Communion. During the homily, the priest reviewed the Ten Commandments with the children. I estimate that this teaching lasted almost forty-five minutes. While the Ten Commandments are indispensable for preparing and forming the consciences of these children, making the Decalogue the focus of the homily was a mistake. It was too long and tended to bore not only the children, but the visiting priests too! I have found it more effective to preach on a short encounter with Jesus and the children, such as when Jesus took the children into his arms and said, "Let the children come to me; do not prevent them, for the kingdom of God belongs to such as these" (Mk. 10:14). In preaching on this text, I would emphasize Jesus' love and mercy for children then, but also now. I encourage the children: "Don't be afraid to confess your sins to the priest because he wants you to come to know and love Jesus." I would then briefly review how to go to confession with them. Often, I give them the same penance, such as pray one our Father or do one good deed for someone. Catechists would distribute a short guide about how to go to confession, which would contain an act of contrition. I think it is important for priests to acknowledge the fear most of the children have. Be welcoming and merciful not only in the homily, but also in the role of confessor. The children need to know that you love them.

What is unique to Hispanic Catholicism and the Sacrament of Reconciliation is the central role the sacrament plays in the life of the faithful. Although the reception of the sacrament went into decline after Vatican II among European American Catholics and has not recovered, Hispanic immigrants in the United States still seek the grace of this sacramental encounter. Hispanics know deep down that they should make a good confession at least once a year. If they haven't confessed their sins to a priest in this way, they know something is lacking in their lives. Long lines outside the confessional are not uncommon in a shared parish with a large Latino population. The popularity of Confession puts extra strain on the priests. Bishops and personnel boards should account for this added burden when making assignments to parishes of the diocese.

Before considering Confirmation, I would like to promote having continuous faith formation between first Communion and Confirmation. Children and their parents need ongoing formation and so there should not be a five-year gap between periods of sacramental preparation. Normally our students begin to prepare for Confirmation at age fourteen and complete the two-year preparation at age fifteen. We follow the same approach of *catechesis familiar* (family catechesis) and require the parents to attend a class at the same time their teenagers are taking a class. I am impressed by the commitment of the catechists, who give their time and talent to these students. I think their love for the Lord and the Church are attractive to our teenagers. They pass their faith on by the witness of their lives.

The climax of the preparation is the celebration of Confirmation at the cathedral with the bishop. Other parishes with Hispanic youth usually accompany our parish. As with Baptism and first Communion, the godparents are present supporting their *ahijados* (godchildren). Although fewer parents are present with their children than at Baptism and first Communion, many still value having their children receive all the sacraments of initiation. This is a motivating factor for Hispanic parents. The deep symbolism of the oil of sacred chrism too speaks to the Hispanic mindset of the need to be touched by the holy love of God, revealed by the flames of the mighty fire of Pentecost.

The audience for this preaching manual includes bishops. How should a bishop preach and preside at a Confirmation for Latinos? In over twenty-three years of Hispanic ministry, I have observed bishops preaching and presiding at Confirmations. In two archdioceses I have witnessed different pastoral practices for bishops. In one, the bishop visits the parish; in the other the *confirmandi*, godparents, parents, and family make the trek to the cathedral, often with other shared parishes with large groups of Hispanic youth. The first practice is by far more effective because it is more personal and pastoral for the bishop to arrive early, share a meal with the parish, celebrate the Rite of Confirmation, and attend a party afterwards. Having five to eight parishes gather in a cathedral is too large a group for the bishop to be personal. This different and unfamiliar setting affects how the preaching is received.

In the cathedral setting, an auxiliary bishop once preached a moral harangue about not having sex before marriage. Although chastity is an important message, the bishop should not have focused on this. This approach to preaching gives the impression that the Church is all about "Thou shall not," instead of focusing on "Thou shall" (love God and neighbor).

At another Confirmation, the auxiliary bishop told the Hispanic youth the story of his own conversion. This personal message effectively communicated the gospel to the *confirmandi*. They listened attentively and could hear themselves in his story. The bishop spoke about how he was always small of stature and how this affected his relationships with others and with God. His vulnerability spoke to the vulnerability of these youth. He talked too about how he had drifted away from the Lord only to come back to him in this college years. The bishop was effective because he followed the method of preaching as testimony. Latinos want to hear about how God is working in the lives of their leaders. As the bishop said, "God did this for me," the youth can envision that God can do the same for them as well.

Another success story was the preaching of the archbishop. He used a cell phone as a prop and talked about how God wants to communicate with us. He began his homily talking about how he was planning to buy a new cell phone and about which features he should get in the new model. Immediately, he grabbed the attention of the youth with this "hook." Then he moved to the heart of the homily: God wants to communicate with you because he loves you. This message was positive and hopeful. The archbishop's style of delivering the message was the most effective I've seen because he walked up and down the aisles of the enormous cathedral and asked the youth questions. His preaching was a conversation with the *confirmandi*. May I be so bold to say to our bishops: Your excellencies, when you preach, please have a conversation with our young people. You will be surprised at how they respond.

One last piece of advice: don't just speak in English. All of the preaching at Confirmations has tended to be in English. Perhaps the bishops think rightly that all the Hispanic youth understand English because that's what they speak at school. That's true, but it's not what all of them speak at home. Moreover, preaching in English indicates that the bishop is ignoring the parents and godparents who may prefer to hear the gospel proclaimed in

THE SACRAMENTS IN YOUTH 79

their native language. I do think that the homily should address both groups of people: the *confirmandi* in English and the rest of the crowd in Spanish. This could involve bilingual preaching in which the bishop first addresses the *confirmandi* and then the parents and godparents. The bishop could alternate between English and Spanish or could divide the homily in two with the first half in English directed to the Hispanic youth and the second half in Spanish directed toward parents and godparents. The bishop should try to nourish all present with the word of God.

The *quinceañera* remains an important ritual within the Hispanic community, although it seems to be practiced unevenly. The reason I say this is that many faithful Hispanic Catholic parents do not emphasize this custom, and so their fifteen-year-old daughters do not request it. Often those who do request the rite are the inactive Hispanic Catholics. What is a *quinceañera*? It is a rite of passage for a fifteen-year-old Hispanic young lady in which she renews her baptismal promises and receives a blessing from the priest. Lavish displays of fashionable hoop skirts, a train of *chambelanes*,[7] the presence of godparents, often a limousine, and a big party are the order of the day. Pastors often complain that such a large amount of money is spent on the *quinceañera*, and the family puts little or no money in the collection basket. It should be noted, however, that the reason the family is able to spend this money is because the godparents and others in the community have pitched in together. This expensive celebration is an expression of the family's love for their daughter. The liturgical rite leads to the celebration of a banquet and dance in honor of the *quinceañera*. It is truly life in the subjunctive!

Source: Photo by Håkon Grimstad on Unsplash.

How should one preach at a *quinceañera*? The preacher must make a conscious effort to help the audience to focus on what is important, such a lavish celebration can be easily distracting. Sometimes, people pay more attention to how they and others are dressed than to the liturgical celebration and spiritual elements. Consequently, I suggest focusing the homily on these

---

7 The *chambelanes* are usually male friends of the young lady and they wear matching suits at the ceremony, walk in procession, and sit together for the entire Mass.

three themes or choosing one or two of them: (1) the love of the family for the *quinceañera*; (2) Mary the Mother of God as an example and model for the young woman; and (3) the renewal of the baptismal vows.

At a *quinceañera*, a young woman's family puts their fifteen-year-old daughter front and center before God and the Hispanic community. They are giving thanks to God for her. This is a cultural way of expressing how special she is to them. These are the reasons for the expenses incurred, including a hoop dress, a limousine, a mariachi band, the outfits for the *chambelanes*, renting a hall, food and drink, and the music for dancing. The homilist can draw attention to how our families shape and form us. Good parents and godparents are gifts from God because they teach and train us to enter into adulthood and to assume our roles within the family and society. Giving thanks to God for family and parents can serve as the main theme for a *quinceañera* homily.

The preacher could also emphasize Mary and her role in salvation history. Focusing on the mystery of the Annunciation is a good strategy. Mary is very much like a fifteen-year-old girl when the angel Gabriel appears to her and announces that she will become mother of the Savior. She is full of grace and is blessed among women. Her response to the angel serves as a model for the *quinceañera*: "Behold, I am a handmaid of the Lord. May it be done to me according to your word" (Lk. 1:38). Mary serves not only as an example to follow; she is also our spiritual mother. She intercedes for the *quinceañera* and her family. Later in the rite, the fifteen-year-old will process to the statue of Our Lady of Guadalupe and present a bouquet of flowers to her. She will implore her motherly help and care for herself and her loved ones.

The last point to highlight is the *quinceañera's* renewal of her baptismal vows. The preacher could refer back to the girl's baptism when her parents and godparents made baptismal vows on behalf of their newborn child. Now, fifteen years later, it is her turn to make that commitment for herself. The parents and godparents have made commitments for the well-being of their daughter, but now it is time for her to take responsibility and give back to her parents, godparents, and family. She steps forward to begin to assume the role of a young woman seeking what is best of all the members of her family.

Unfortunately, after Confirmation and the *quinceañera*, many Hispanic youth and young adults move away from the Church until they decide to get married. The research shows that both Anglo and Hispanic young adult Catholics tend to drift away from their faith. The same is true for Protestant Anglo young adults. The only group of youth and young adults that does not fall away from the faith is Latino Protestants. One particular emphasis for this group is to have regular youth and young adult ministries and meetings. They also encourage Latino young adults to assume leadership positions in these groups and ministries.[8] In summary, Latino Protestants are ahead of Latino Catholics because these communities invest time, energy, and resources in their Hispanic youth and young adults. Catholic parishes and dioceses would be wise to follow their example.

For another view, the *V Encuentro* in Dallas from September 20–23, 2018 featured young adult Latino Catholics. Attending the *V Encuentro* with a staff member and a Latina young adult, I had the opportunity to listen to young adult Latinos and Latinas as they spoke about their hopes and dreams. In conversations, worship, prayer, and fun, they demonstrated their love and commitment for the Lord and the Catholic Church. They also voiced their concerns. They want adults to accompany them in their walk with the Lord in his Catholic Church. They want more opportunities for formation, education, and spaces for ministry. These young adults presented a much more hopeful picture for the present and future of Hispanic Catholics than what the statistics show.[9]

Questions for Reflection and Discussion

1. Have you attended a Hispanic baptism? Discuss what you noticed. Why are Latinos attracted to baptism and to first Communion?

2. What would be a good pastoral plan for parents who seek these two sacraments for their children but otherwise are inactive Catholics?

3. Have you ever attended a Confirmation of Hispanic youth? Discuss what you noticed.

4. What did you learn about *quinceañeras*? Are they offered in your parish?

---

[8] *Pathways of Hope and Faith Among Hispanic Teens: Pastoral Reflections and Strategies Inspired by the National Study of Youth and Religion*, ed. Ken Johnson-Mondragon (Stockton, CA: Instituto Fe y Vida, 2007), 280–81.

[9] For a detailed report on the *V Encuentro*, see *V National Encuentro of Hispanic/Latino Ministry: Missionary Disciples: Witnesses of God's Love; Working Document* (Washington, DC: USCCB, 2018).

Hispanic Sacramentality and the Sacraments in Adulthood

Marriage and family represent the core of Hispanic life. Most Latinos will have a family. This is central to their identity. The sorrows and joys of Latinos center around the family. If their marriage and family life are going well, Latinos are happy, despite problems with health, work, and employment. If marital difficulties and problems raising children dominate their lives, Latinos become saddened, no matter what kind of success they experience at work and in society. Family and its commitments are the heart of Hispanic culture.

Hispanic sacramentality means that God is revealed in the web of relationships of family. Each person in the family is a sacrament in that he or she reveals the divine.[1] Every person is created in God's image and likeness, and every person in the Hispanic family is acknowledged as special for this reason. Celebrations of sacraments, birthdays, and other milestones provide Latinos with the occasions to celebrate life in the subjunctive.

Latinos requesting marriage preparation and reception of the Sacrament of Matrimony are usually cohabitating or civilly married. The majority have been together for ten or twenty years, have already given birth to children, and raised them. They sense something is missing because they have not yet received the Sacrament of Marriage. Often this realization comes when their children are in first Communion classes. The children ask them, "*Pape, Mame, porque no comulgas?*" ("Dad, Mom, why don't *you* receive the Eucharist?") We encourage our parishioners to receive the Eucharist only if they are in sacramental marriages, although we try to give people room to follow their consciences on this intimate matter. Just as the children bring their

---

1 Goizueta, *Caminemos*, 48–53.

parents to Church on Sunday for faith formation, so too they often bring their parents to the sacramental marriage. Jesus reminds us: "Amen, I say to you, unless you become like children, you will not enter the kingdom of heaven" (Mt 18:3). In the Hispanic community, children have an important role in drawing their parents closer to the Lord and to the Church.

Many factors bring Hispanic couples to the decision to become married in the Church. We try to listen closely, not only in their first meeting with the priest as they fill out paperwork but in their ongoing preparation with classes and mentor couples. We usually require a five to six-month formation period for these couples. This is a time of grace for them. Many are learning about their faith for the first time. Many are starting to attend Mass every Sunday. As the things of God become more a part of their marriage and family, they grow in contentment.

The wedding ceremony is the culmination of this marriage preparation, and it is day of great joy for the couple. Their *padrinos* (godparents), parents, children, relatives, friends, and coworkers accompany them on this special day. The wedding ceremony is filled with rich symbols that resonate with Hispanic sacramentality: the wedding clothes—a nice suit for the groom and a white, long wedding dress for the bride—the rings, the *arras* (coins), the *lazo* (the wedding cord), a Bible, and a rosary. As the wedding begins, the bride radiant in a white wedding dress meets the groom in the front of the church, the parents bless her, and give her to the groom. This is an important exchange at the beginning of the Mass with which the presider will not want to interfere. This custom is deeply embedded in Hispanic traditions and culture. After the Liturgy of the Word, the Marriage Rite is celebrated. The exchange of rings follows the exchange of the words of consent. The wedding ring is polyvalent symbol representing commitment, faithfulness, tenderness, the marriage covenant, passion, respect, eternity, and love.

The *arras* (coins) and the *lazo* (wedding cord) originate in the Visigothic wedding customs from the Iberian peninsula that influenced marriage customs in Spain. Missionaries from Spain then brought these practices to the New World where they blended with the customs of the indigenous populations.[2] One example of inculturation is parallels between Aztec wedding customs and those of the Spanish: "When an Aztec couple wed, they sat on separate mats, which were then joined by tassels to signify their marital union. In addition, the groom's family bestowed gifts on the bride. These practices mirror the Visigothic Spanish traditions of joining the couple by a

---

2 Timothy Matovina, "Marriage Celebrations in Mexican-American Communities," in *Mestizo Worship: A Pastoral Approach to Liturgical Ministry*, authored by Timothy Matovina and Virgilio Elizondo (Collegeville, MN: Liturgical Press, 1998), 96–97.

lazo and the groom presenting a marital pledge or *arras*."[3] In today's Hispanic weddings, the groom holds the *arras* (coins) in his hands above the opened hands of the bride. He promises to share the material blessings received with his wife. Having received the *arras* (coins), the bride then repeats the action, promising to share their goods mutually.

The placing of the *lazo* (a wedding cord) occurs after the presider has blessed the *lazo*. He also may bless additional religious objects at this time, including a Bible, a rosary, pillows, and flowers. At this point, I usually direct the couple to kneel on two kneelers in front of the church, and then the godparents drape the *lazo* (wedding cord) around the bride and the groom. Once again, the *lazo* and this ritual action are powerful polyvalent symbols which mean many things, such as indissolubility, faithfulness, unity, relationship, sharing, protection, and family. Another symbol common at Hispanic weddings is the lighting of a marriage unity candle and then the signing of their marriage certificate. The presider, however, should not forget the couple's procession to the image of Our Lady of Guadalupe. One of their first acts as a married couple is to entrust themselves and their family to her motherly help and care. The bride offers her a bouquet of roses, symbolizing her commitment to her. Mary serves as the model for the Hispanic woman in her roles as both wife and mother.

How should the presider preach at a Hispanic wedding? I tend to preach catechetically or mystagogically on these occasions. Mystagogy involves drawing attention to the rite and then unpacking its meaning for the gathered assembly. I often highlight the exchange of consent as a sacramental moment that brings about the unity of a man and woman in the bond of marriage. The rings, the *arras*, and the *lazo* provide further material for the homilist to explain. These symbols and their accompanying ritual actions speak deeply to Latinos.

My wedding homilies, however, usually tend to be more catechetical. Starting from the Scriptures, I talk about how the institution of marriage comes from God in the beginning when he created Adam and Eve. The first man describes the first woman as bone from my bone and flesh from my flesh. The two become one in marriage. Then I ask the question, "What does it mean to say that marriage is a sacrament?" Sacraments are the union of heaven and earth. For example, in Baptism water comes from the earth and the Holy Spirit descends from heaven. When the children enter into the water of baptism, they are filled with power from on high. The Eucharist brings together bread and wine from the earth, and the Holy Spirit from heaven transforms the bread and wine into the body and blood of Christ.

---

3 Matovina, "Marriage Celebrations," 97.

"What about marriage?" I ask. "What comes from heaven and what comes from the earth?" I talk about human love between the couple coming from the earth. At this moment on this special day, both the man and the woman are recognizing that something is lacking in their human love: they do not yet have the love of God poured out from heaven upon their human love. That will happen at the moment the couple exchanges consent.

I conclude the Hispanic wedding homily by asking what the couple needs to practice so that their marriages go well. Communication, trust, respect, and affection are among the answers people give. I usually focus on three pieces of advice. First, couples need to learn how to forgive each other and how to ask for forgiveness. St. Paul recommends: "Be angry but do not sin; do not let the sun set on your anger" (Eph. 4:26). How many problems could married couples avoid if they just practiced asking for forgiveness and granting pardon to each other? I jokingly say a husband or a wife would often rather die than say these nine words in English or seven words in Spanish: I am sorry (*Lo siento*); I was wrong (*Estoy equivocado*); please forgive me (*Favor de perdonarme*). When a spouse says these words, the proper response is "Yes, my love, I forgive you" (*Si, mi amor, te perdono*). Then I have everyone repeat these words.

Further advice for the couple includes anticipating my spouse's needs and focusing on good memories with one's beloved. Anticipating what my spouse needs takes the focus off of me and my needs. This refocusing of the spouse's attention helps them both to overcome selfishness. If all I think about is myself and my needs, then I will have trouble living out the marriage commitment. I conclude my advice by asking them two questions: "How many have good memories from our time together with our beloved? How many have bad memories?" I ask them to raise their hands in response to these questions. I tell them that I will close my eyes so as not to see who is raising their hands answering the second question. If we are honest, we will admit that we all have both good and bad memories, but we can choose to focus on the good memories by setting the bad memories aside and leaving them in the past. This choice of how we think about our spouse will give us greater affection. Couples have found this advice helpful.

Nevertheless, like everyone, Latinos experience brokenness in their marriages and families. The Sacrament of Reconciliation serves as a means to bring forgiveness, healing, and strength to faltering marriages and to family members experiencing strife. Women in particular often confess their own sins along with the sins of the rest of the family—at times forgetting the former! I refer back to our exploration of sacramentality and how Latinos view the person as a sacrament. Each person in the family represents the whole family. The sins of one become the sins of the family as a whole in the

Hispanic worldview. Latinos know they are sinners in need of God's grace, and for this reason, they frequently confess their sins in this sacrament. In Euro-American culture a lack of sense of sin is not uncommon. This does not extend to first generation Hispanic immigrants, although second and third generation immigrants are beginning to display this trend of an impoverished sense of sin. First generation Hispanic immigrants, on the other hand, need to know the promise of God's mercy, forgiveness, and power to transform even the most broken marriage and home. They need hope that things can get better.

The symbols and ritual actions of the Sacrament of Reconciliation are powerful. First, the confessional provides privacy so that penitents can confess their sins to the priest and to God with confidentiality. The posture of kneeling embodies an act of repentance. One kneels, moved by humility and sorrow, and confesses one's shortcomings. Most confessions are heartfelt, and penitents show contrition. Sometimes mothers and fathers, however, force their children to go to the Sacrament of Penance. In these circumstances, I try to help them make a good confession by asking the children questions. At times, I help them form their consciences by reviewing some of the Ten Commandments. In the confessional at my parish, I have taped an image of Jesus embracing a sinner as they together walk along a beach. On this image is an act of contrition in Spanish. If the penitents can read Spanish, I encourage them to make this act of contrition. Some, however, know a longer form by memory, which I permit them to pray. Then I extend my hand and give them absolution, forgiving them their sins. This action too is powerful in that it symbolizes a forgiveness of sins and reconciliation with God and the Church.

What is unique to Hispanic Catholicism is the women's type of confession. In Hispanic culture, women bear the responsibility of handing on the faith and culture to their children. Single women often share this call as godmothers. Wives and mothers, however, feel this burden more deeply. When their children or husbands sin, they feel that it is their sin. The Confessor should gently remind them that they are responsible before the Lord for their own sins, but not for the sins of their husbands and children. When listening to many Hispanic women confessing their sins, the priest will become aware of the strain these women endure and realize that they may need help outside the sacrament. Some suffer abuse and post-traumatic stress disorder. Some are frustrated. Some are depressed. All of this comes out. Hispanics use the term "*deshogarse*," which means "unburden," "blow off steam," "give vent to" or "spilling one's guts." Tears, sobbing, and expressions of grief will accompany many confessions. The priest will become accustomed to this phenomena and seek to bring the healing of Christ to these women in pain. He should help the woman make a good confession by focusing on a thorough examination of conscience and confession of sin—and not on therapy. A merciful, kind confessor can do an enormous amount of good in the confessional in reconciling the Hispanic Catholic woman to God and the Church.

In addition to sin, sickness is another cause of brokenness. When serious illness strikes, Latinos will often tell me about it after Mass and ask for prayer with *"los santos oleos"* (the holy oils). They pour out their hearts to me telling me about cancer, heart problems, back and knee pain, headaches, diabetes, and more. I usually instruct them to bring their family to the front of the church where the holy oils are kept to the left of the altar. I open the glass cabinet and find the oil of the sick. I tell them to wait while I go to the sacristy for the *Rite of Pastoral Care of the Sick and Dying*. I find the short rite for anointing in an Institution or Hospital, and then begin the prayer over the sick. I place my hands on the sick, praying in silence for their healing and strength. Then I anoint the sick on the forehead, palms, and wherever they hurt, such as neck or leg, or face (I try to use good discretion and modesty here so as not to make someone feel uncomfortable). After praying an Our Father, a closing prayer, and giving a final blessing, I encourage them to give one another the sign of peace.

Touching is a powerful symbol highlighted in the Anointing of the Sick. The priest touches the head as he lays his hands on the sick and prays for healing and strength. Then he touches the forehead, the palms, and the sick areas of the body. Touch is so important for the sick because then they know they are not alone as they face their sickness. They have Christ, the Church, and their family to strengthen them, pray for them, and bring them healing. The Covid-19 pandemic resulted in a lack of touching, leading to a lack of connection with others. This phenomenon was extended to the Sacrament of the Sick and was an often-unnoticed burden shared by all Catholics, but especially by Latinos because of the very physical nature of their cultural forms of greeting and communication.

Most anointings occur after Mass. Nevertheless, Latinos will not hesitate to call me to the hospital in the event of an emergency. Most of the first-generation immigrants tend to be healthy and so if they are in the hospital, it is usually a serious accident or the onset of an illness. First-generation immigrants too will invite their elderly parents to live with them in the U.S.; at times they will become sick and die. The cross-cultural preacher must be sensitive to the Hispanic worldview of death and dying.

Death is the final area of exploration for Hispanic sacramentality in the span of a lifetime. My experience of Hispanic ministry has involved middle-aged, first-generation immigrants and their children. Most of their parents are in their country of origin, although some of their elderly parents immigrate to the U.S. and reside with their grown-up children. One of the first deaths in my first assignment was the drowning of a young boy who waded out into the cold water of a mountain river, got in over his head, could not swim, and drowned. I went to comfort the family of the deceased child. They were crying and mourning openly; they were not speaking Spanish, but an indigenous language from Mexico, probably from Oaxaca. I really did not know what to do other than to be there as the presence of the Lord and his Church, helping them in this terrible tragedy. Unfortunately, tragedies, such as drownings, car accidents, or homicides, do occur and the preacher and pastoral workers must be available and helpful to the families in these difficult times. Also in this category of unexpected deaths are heart attacks, still born babies, and other accidents. I have found reading Psalm 23 and calling attention to the Lord as our shepherd to be consoling in times of tragedy.

The death of the elderly is more common among Anglos in the shared parish. Although difficult, these types of deaths are easier than unexpected or premature death. Long, drawn-out illnesses, such as cancer, also occur among Latinos. The important thing is to accompany the Hispanic family at this time and to console them. Latinos have the custom of giving the bereaved person *la* pésame (condolences). I usually try to do this individually with family members by looking them in the eye and shaking their hands and sincerely saying, *Te doy la pésame* (I give you condolences). This is also a best practice for a funeral homily.

Latinos have healthier cultural resources to deal with death and dying than do most Anglos. Latinos remember their deceased loved ones annually on *el día de los muertos* (the Day of the Dead) on November 2, the Feast of All Souls. They have the custom of building small altars in their homes or church buildings. They place pictures of their dead friends and family members upon these altars, along with other items to remember them, such as their favorite dish (*pozole, menudo, o tamales*), their preferred drink *tequila o cerveza como corona* (tequila or beer like corona), their religious items (rosaries or medals), and other objects. Latinos tell stories of the lives of their deceased loved ones, pray for their eternal rest, and enjoy good food and company on this special day. Death, therefore, is not something to be avoided, feared, or done away with. It is not something to be dealt with just near the end of someone's earthly existence. Rather, death accompanies Latinos throughout the course of life. The Hispanic culture regularly reminds people of the reality of death and encourages them to be ready for it when it comes.

Hispanic sacramentality causes Latinos to have a special love for the body of the deceased. Whereas Anglos try to avoid a dead body by closing it up in a casket and merely having a glimpse of the corpse dressed up in a suit or dress, Latinos come close to the body of the deceased, often touching or kissing the face of the beloved. The person is embodied in the cadaver for the

Source: RubeHM, CC BY-SA 4.0, via Wikimedia Commons.

Hispanic mind, and so they approach the body with love and affection. Such lavish expressions of sorrow and humanity are ubiquitous at the Hispanic vigil.

I remember one time when the family did not want the casket to close. The funeral director did not follow my directive that the casket needed to be closed at the beginning of the funeral Mass and not reopened afterwards. Much to my consternation, he reopened it at the request of the family. This action led the family and friends to an awkward period in which they pleaded with the funeral director not to close the casket. An important moment of closure in the rite was lost. Another custom which demonstrates Hispanic sacramentality is the burial rite at the cemetery. Latinos will often participate in the burial by each putting a shovel of dirt on the casket. This is an embodied rite that shows closure and reminds us of the words from Scripture spoken to us when we receive ashes at the beginning of Lent: "Remember that you are dust, and to dust you shall return."[4] Other traditions include the nine-day novena for the deceased. This practice usually consists of praying the Rosary at the funeral home or in the family's home. Clergy can attend these, but ordinarily the family can lead these prayers. Latinos will also offer Masses in the parish for the eternal rest for those who have died.

Latinos have a deep belief in eternal life after death and in their communion with the lives of the deceased. This faith is deeply engrained in both first-generation immigrants and their parents. Their children, however, do not necessarily share these beliefs unless their parents and grandparents have passed them on to them. There is a great need to evangelize and catechize second and third generation Hispanic Catholics about fundamental beliefs on life and death, including heaven, hell, purgatory, the last judgment, the Communion of Saints and the resurrection from the dead. As these children of the first-generation immigrants become more secular and Euro-American in their worldview, they are in danger of losing these core tenets of Catholic belief and practice.

First generation immigrants need to be reminded of these things as well, but they have deep faith. What they need is the catechesis that can give them more understanding. Although they are adults, their faith level may be only at the maturity of an eight-year-old having just made his or her first Communion. When someone dies, Latinos need to be taught clearly what the Church teaches and expects. For example, the funeral liturgy has three parts: the vigil, the funeral Mass, and the committal at the cemetery. Most Latinos do not know this basic framework for approaching the funeral rites of the deceased. Regular catechesis around *el día de los muertos* on November 2 would be a wise practice. The cross-cultural preacher to Latinos can provide some basic catechesis in the homily, focusing on grief and consolation, life after death, the Communion of Saints, and the resurrection. These master themes can guide preachers as they try to connect the Word of God with the life of the deceased and the gathered liturgical assembly as they celebrate the Eucharist.

I have led you on a journey through the span of a lifetime of Latinos as they manifest their sacramentality in the celebration of the sacraments. Beginning with a prayer over the unborn child in the womb of a Hispanic mother and ending with the funeral rites for the death of a loved one, I hope

---

[4] *The Roman Missal: English Translation According to the Third Typical Edition* (Catholic Book Publishing Corp.: New Jersey, 2011), 72. See also Gen. 3:19.

I have shown the richness of these embodied rituals and symbols. Next, I will move to the sacramentality of time as it is expressed in the course of one year.

Questions for Reflection and Discussion

1. Have you been to a Hispanic wedding? What observations do you have? What did you understand or not understand?
2. The celebration of weddings represents life celebrated in the subjunctive. What does this mean?
3. Marriage and family are central to the identity of Hispanics. What are your observations?
4. Have you experienced death and dying among Latinos? How is their approach different from the Anglo-American approach toward death and dying?

10

Hispanic Sacramentality in the Span of the Liturgical Year

I want to begin this chapter by relating a pastoral success story. By explaining what has worked well in my parish, I hope to convey to you good ideas and best practices so that you can choose wisely, experiment, and find out what works for your parish. I noticed that our 6:00 pm Mass was the least attended of our Spanish Masses, averaging between 150 and 170 people. In comparison, the other two Spanish Masses have a regular crowd of 400 or 500 people. A previous pastor started this 6:00 pm Mass for Latinos who work on Sundays. Many work in service industries that require Sunday work. Therefore, unless the parish offers Mass at a convenient time, they will not be able to attend. Although this liturgy had regular attendance, a choir, and faithful lectors, extraordinary ministers of Holy Communion, altar servers, and ushers, something was lacking. I did not perceive a great deal of joy, hope, or energy coming from this Mass. Part of the reason, I thought, was that this Mass does not follow the pattern of our other Spanish masses which include faith formation. At the other two liturgies, parents and their children have classes before Mass. What could I do to bring more energy, life, and people to the 6:00 pm Spanish mass?

In August 2019, I began to meet with Miguel, Pablo, Maria, Rosario, and David about what we could do to draw more people into our life at our parish by attending Mass on Sunday at 6:00 pm. Together we formed a committee with the purpose of doubling the attendance of this Mass by August 2020. I appointed Miguel to serve as chairman and Pablo to be his assistant. Together we decided to increase Mass attendance by focusing on three areas to find a theme for each Mass: popular religion, location, and work. Usually, popular religion and location come together in people's customs and traditions.

For example, the people of Mexico honor Our Lady of Guadalupe: location (Mexico) and popular piety from centuries of practice come together. Next, we began to work on a "Hispanic Liturgical Calendar." At times, our calendar would correspond with the official calendar of the Roman Catholic Church, but at other times it would vary, depending on what draws Latinos to church. We made a list of the most common types of work that Latinos do, including cleaning, landscaping, construction, restaurants, roofing, hotels, and such. We also consulted Appendix I of the *Misal Romano, Tercera Edición*—USA Edition. The patronal feasts for 20 Hispanic countries are listed there along with the date of the celebration. For example, Argentina celebrates the Blessed Virgin Mary de Lujan on May 8th. We underscored those countries that our parish demographics include: Mexico, Ecuador, El Salvador, Honduras, Guatemala, Peru, and Colombia. Then we got to work establishing a calendar specific to our Hispanic community. We also divided up responsibilities for advertising the Mass and finding Mass coordinators. Last, we agreed to meet every two weeks at 5 pm to review and plan for the future.

What have been the results? We began our first special Mass according to the Hispanic liturgical calendar on September 22, 2020, by celebrating San Nicolas Tolentino. This saint's day is a popular celebration in Tolentino in the state of Puebla in the country of Mexico. The promotors of this tradition were dressed in festive yellow garments and carried a statue of San Nicolas in procession at the beginning of Mass. They also brought loaves of bread in baskets and placed them at the side on the statue in front of the altar. At the beginning of Mass, I enthusiastically greeted all the parishioners along with these special guests. At the end of Mass, they processed out with the liturgical ministers and distributed loaves of bread to the faithful at the entrance of the church. Mass attendance was more than usual because of this special event. We were off to a good start.

Source: Public domain.

The following week we celebrated the feast of the Archangels. This feast day was superseded by the 26th Sunday in Ordinary Time, which we observed in the celebration of the Mass. Nevertheless, devotees of Saint Michael, Saint Raphael, and Saint Gabriel processed to the altar with statues and images honoring the Archangels. We also included special intercessions to call upon the powerful assistance of these heavenly beings. After processing out of

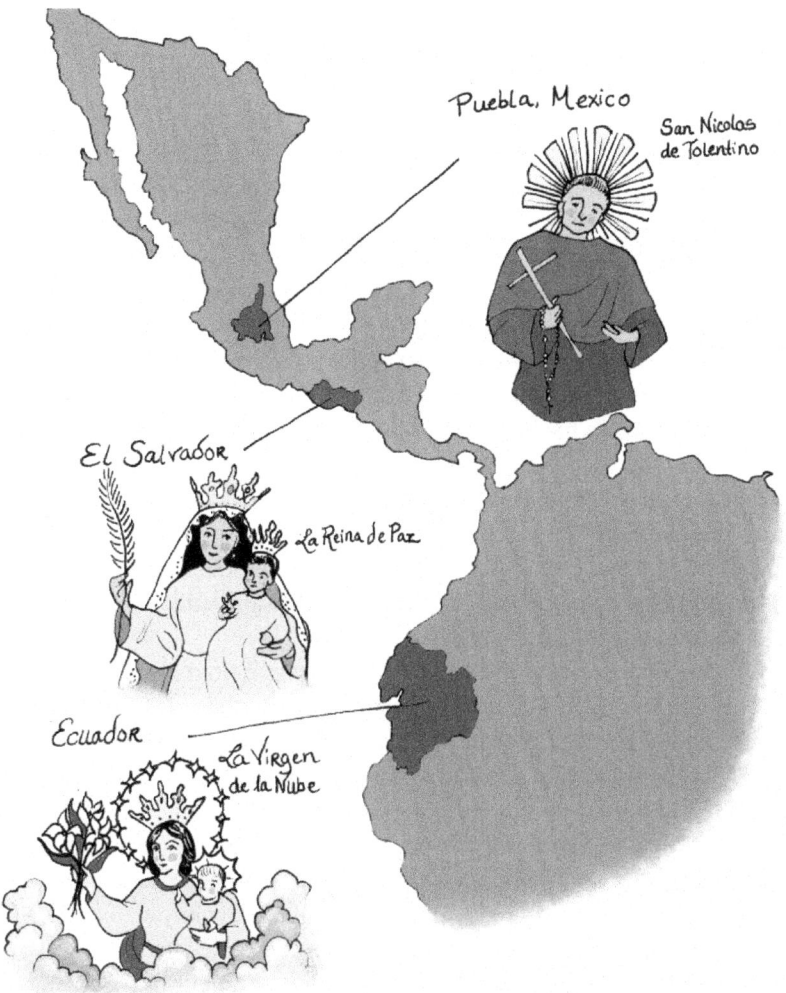

Source: Joanie McMahon.

the main church, many approached asking me to bless their medallions of Saint Michael the Archangel.

The following Sunday we looked to the guidance of the Church's liturgical calendar by highlighting Our Lady of the Rosary, which the Church designates for October 7. Because it fell on a Monday, we moved it back one day to fit our Hispanic liturgical calendar. Rosaries were a common sight on this festive day. Pilgrims carried a large rosary accompanying the altar servers, lectors, and the presider in the procession at the beginning of Mass. I again welcomed all parishioners as well as guests who wanted to honor Our

Lady of the Rosary. In the homily, I drew attention to Mary's motherly help and care and the practice of praying the Rosary.

On the next Sunday, Oct 13, we celebrated our first work Mass in honor of all those who clean. Some cleaners brought their cleaning instruments, such as brooms and brushes, walked in procession, and placed these objects in front of the altar for a blessing. At the end of the Mass, I sprinkled holy water over these tools and then asked all those who clean to stand up for a special blessing. Once again, Mass attendance was up, in part because many of the faithful dedicated to Saint Nicolas Tolentino are cleaners, and we made sure to invite them.

On October 20, we remembered Saint Luke, "transferring" its celebration from Oct. 18th to the following Sunday. We have a history of honoring St. Luke because we have a large population of parishioners from Puebla, Mexico, who are dedicated to this evangelist. For this reason, Mass attendance was greater than usual. This feast day also brings great pageantry to the Church because it is a tradition for the people bring their stature of St. Luke encased in glass and on a throne. They also have banners honoring St. Luke. For the homily, I drew people's attention to this saint and also the imagery present in the statue and the banners.

On the 30th Sunday in Ordinary Time, we invited all landscapers to come and receive a special blessing. Some carried implements such as rakes, clippers, and even a leaf blower, and wanted these tools of their trade to be blessed. Again, we encouraged these landscapers to walk in procession with the priest and to place their work tools in front of the altar. After Mass, the priest then blessed them and their tools by sprinkled holy water on them. In a sense, this second work Mass showed that we were trying to reach out and invite inactive Catholics to come to Mass. If they know that the Mass connects to their daily life and work, they are more likely to attend.

At the beginning of November, we celebrated our third work Mass by inviting construction workers to attend. These workers brought hammers, crowbars, drills, and screw drivers, carried them in procession to the altar and placed them in front of the altar for all to see. During the homily, I drew attention to St. Joseph and Jesus, both who were construction workers! At the end of the Mass, I invited them to stand, extended my arms and prayed a blessing over them before sprinkling holy water on their nonelectrical tools.

We celebrated a special feast day for the people of El Salvador called *La Reina de la Paz* (the Queen of Peace) on Sunday, November 10. The order of the evening events included a video presentation of the feast day at 5:30 pm, followed by Mass at 6 pm, followed by a celebration with food in the church foyer. This was by far the most well attended and successful Mass up until then. What made it successful? The two leaders promoting the event were our maintenance man and a member of the parish finance council. They worked hard getting the word out ahead of time and arrived early to make sure everything was set up correctly so that the evening would be flawless. It was! The church was filled with regular parishioners and over a hundred Salvadorian guests. They were delighted to see their traditions displayed in a Catholic church in the U.S. They were rapt in attention during the video presentation and belted out the song honoring *La Reina de La Paz*. After Mass, they stayed and enjoyed traditional treats from El Salvador.

Source: Via Edwin del Valle, Wikimedia Commons.

Although we focused on popular religion and location the next Sunday, the Mass turnout was less than we expected. We invited the Ecuadorians to honor the Blessed Virgin Mary of the Presentation del Quinche. My hunch is that the Ecuadorians were not as well organized as the Salvadorians because this was their first time for this celebration. Another good question to ask the Ecuadorians would be if this is a common feast day in their country. Although it is listed as a patronal feast day in Appendix I of the Misal Romano,

Source: Rodrigoardiles, CC BY-SA 3.0, via Wikimedia Commons.

it didn't seem like the Ecuadorians I talked to were familiar with this tradition; they were more accustomed to celebrating *La Virgen de las Nubes* (The Virgin of the Clouds) and *La Virgen de la Cisne* (the Virgin of Cisne.)

The following two Sundays we adhered strictly to the church's liturgical calendar in our celebration of *Cristo Rey* (Christ the King) and the First Sunday of Advent. *Cristo Rey* is popular in Mexico because of the example and witness of the Cristeros, especially the martyr Bl. Fr. Miguel Pro, who exclaimed defiantly *"Que Viva Cristo Rey!"* (Long live Christ the King!) just before his execution. Christ the King marks the end of the liturgical year, and the next Sunday is the first Sunday of Advent. The tradition of the advent candles was brought to the U.S. by missionaries from Northern Europe.

Although not Hispanic in origin, the Advent symbols of the wreath and the four candles speak deeply to Hispanic piety. A catechist explained this ritual to parents and their children before Mass began. Each family then made an Advent wreath for home to light the candles in anticipation of the coming of the Lord sacramentally, at Christmas, and at the end of time.

Our best turnout occurred the following Sunday for the celebration of *La Imaculada Concepción de la Virgen* (the Immaculate Conception of the Virgin Mary). Two of our ushers, a married couple, serve at the 6:00 pm Mass. Jose and Virginia come from Jolalpan, Puebla, and the patroness of this town is the Immaculate Conception of the Virgin Mary. They took extra time and effort to organize a beautiful celebration that included young girls in white dresses preforming a dance at 5:00 pm in the church and a Mariachi band before the liturgy. The Mass itself had the best attendance of all the Masses since we started this endeavor to increase Mass attendance at the Sunday 6:00 pm Mass. Although our original goal was to double Mass attendance by the following August, we had already surpassed that. The church was completely full! After Mass, we walked in procession led by pilgrims carrying a statue of the Immaculate Conception of the Virgin Mary. The crowd from Jolalpan, Puebla rented the gymnasium, which they had decorated. We sang songs together as the bands played and afterwards enjoyed a traditional dish from their region in Mexico.

For the Third Sunday in Advent, we chose to continue to honor Our Lady of Guadalupe, celebrated on the Thursday beforehand. Because this feast day is the center of the Hispanic liturgical year, those who could not make it to the church on the twelfth were encouraged to come on this Sunday and sing *Mañanitas* to our Lady of Guadalupe. A Mariachi band provided music to serenade *La Virgen Morenita* (the little, brown-skinned Virgin).

For the Fourth Sunday of Advent, we celebrated *Posadas* after Mass. Again, the attendance was good because the people love this tradition of remembering Joseph and Mary and their search for lodging before Jesus was born. They go from house to house before finally finding someone to take them in. After celebrating *Posadas*, the pilgrims processed to the gym where they enjoyed food and gave candy to the children. The custom is to have a *piñata* at the celebration of the *Posadas*.

Our last celebration of the year followed the liturgical calendar of the Church by honoring the Holy Family. The family and home of the Holy Family speaks deeply to the Hispanic imagination. They want their families to model the family life shown by Joseph, Mary, and Jesus.

These were our parish's efforts to improve attendance at the 6:00 pm Spanish Mass on Sundays. We set the goal of doubling attendance in one year and achieved that goal less than four months. We were successful because what we chose to do resonated with Hispanic sacramentality by focusing on popular religion, location, and work. I look forward to our continuing to bring more inactive Hispanic Catholics to Mass on Sundays. We are trying to give them fifty-two reasons to come to Mass throughout the year. Thus far, we are pleased with the results.

Questions for Reflection and Discussion

1. What do you think of the concept of the Hispanic Liturgical Year? What is it and how does it differ from the Church's liturgical calendar?

2. Are you familiar with any of the celebrations described? Which ones? What are your observations?

3. Is there anything in this chapter that might help your parish or community? What is it and why?

4. How does your parish evangelize and grow? What are you doing that builds up the body of Christ?

11

The Hispanic Moment and Where to Go from Here

To reiterate, the U.S. Catholic Church is experiencing a Hispanic moment. This transformation of the Catholic Church, which is now 43% Hispanic, will only continue in the future. Indeed, 60% of Catholics under the age of eighteen are Hispanic. Rather than see this development as negative, this preaching manual is intended to encourage all to embrace this change as an opportunity to renew the Church. This renewal, however, will require a different mindset on the part of Catholic leadership. Instead of viewing Hispanic sacramentality and popular piety in a pejorative way, leaders should focus on the benefits the Hispanic community brings to the Body of Christ. These fruits manifest themselves foremost in a heightened sense of sacramentality, a worldview Latinos express in popular piety.

Still, where do we go from here? It would be a waste of time and effort to have your knowledge remain at a theoretical level. To embrace the Hispanic moment, it is necessary to make plans to implement what you learned and make it real in your daily life. In this final chapter, I will offer suggestions as I review the benefits of the Hispanic moment.

The intense popular piety of Latinos is revealed in popular religion, meaning the religious practices of the people. These include pilgrimages to shrines, prayers for the souls in purgatory, and the use of sacramentals (water, oil, candles). These actions are family and lay centered and take place in the home, often led by the *abuelas* (the grandmothers). The Catholic faith has been handed on from one generation to the next primarily by these practices of popular religion. The gospel has become inculturated in the devotions brought from Spain by missionaries as they blended with the religious practices of the indigenous people. A new *mestizaje* (mixture) has taken place, one that is alive and vibrant and capable of being passed on. Take time to visit a Hispanic home and witness expressions of popular piety, such as the rosary or small altar in the home. Invite parishioners in small groups to share their religious practices at home. As you hear about these devotions, affirm them; talk about how good they are and how they can lead to worship of the Eucharist on Sundays.

Popular religion is accessible to all people: hence, its lasting value and its ability to be transmitted from parents and grandparents to their children. This living faith offers itself as a mutual enrichment for the official liturgy of the Church expressed in the celebration of the Eucharist. While the latter is the Big Story, the former is the collection of little stories that often originate among the poor and the marginalized. When the Church respects and honors and welcomes the popular piety of the people, the Big Story benefits. When the Church neglects, rejects or belittles the little stories, the Big Story of the Tradition manifested in the liturgy tends to lose its relevance to the daily lives of the people. Have you taken time to hear the little stories of your immigrants? What are they? What are the most cherished practices of popular religion in your parish? Organize a retreat day to focus on popular religion and the little stories of the immigrants in your parish community.

Because the origins of Hispanic popular piety are from the Iberian peninsula and are pre-Trent, the Catholicism brought to the New World by the missionaries was medieval and baroque, and therefore not affected by the rationalism and analytical aspects of the Council of Trent. This worldview expressed itself in the senses: elaborate religious processions, sacramentals, beautiful, sensuous churches, and lots of art. The Church in North America, however, was founded by Northern European missionaries very much influenced by the Council of Trent: hence, the focus on precision, doctrine, and exact formulation of the faith to protect and define the institution of the Church against the attack of Protestantism. By understanding this history, Catholic religious leaders can look to Hispanic popular piety to retrieve a lost part of our Tradition. This retrieval can inspire a deeper, more profound sacramental intuition for greater participation and reverence for the sacramental life of the Church. What is your attitude toward popular religion? What about your parish? What do you value in it? Do you see it as having the potential to enrich the celebration of the Eucharist and the sacraments? Meet with your liturgical ministers to talk about retrieving a lost part of Catholic Tradition and how this can enrich the liturgy. Interview some of your immigrants and ask them to share their experiences of Sunday worship.

Retrieving Tradition can be way of gaining a more profound understanding of ecclesiology so that the U.S. Catholic Church can become a missionary church. The period from the Council of Trent (1545–63) until

Vatican I (1869–70) is marked by an overemphasis on the Church's institutional identity. This deformation leads to clericalism. Fostering the popular religion of the Hispanic community is a safeguard against institutionalism and clericalism in the Church. Hispanic popular piety has the potential to renew the church by helping her focus on what is essential. She is called to be close to the people, particularly the poor and the marginalized. Pope Francis wants the Church to be poor for the poor. It's worth asking ourselves how close we are to the poor and marginalized in our parish or diocese. Find out who are the poor and visit them. Follow Pope Francis's advice and go to the peripheries. Most likely you will find many are Latinos.

The Hispanic moment gives us the opportunity for a more profound understanding of sacramentality. This involves paying closer attention to symbols and how they reveal and communicate God's grace to people. The two central symbols for Latinos are the crucified Christ and Mary, his mother. A statue or image of either is a window to the divine. When a Hispanic woman kisses the cross or the feet of the crucified Christ, she is kissing Christ himself in his Passion and Death. The particular reveals the universal and makes the universal present, alive, and efficacious. This deep sacramentality pervades the Hispanic worldview and extends to their understanding of the person, the family, and the community.

For Latinos, the person is sacrament. Each individual person represents a web of relationships: father, mother, grandmother, grandfather, brother, sister, cousin. A person is never alone but always part of a family. All these relationships make the Hispanic person who she or he is. He or she is the sum of all these relationships. This family-centered worldview is enlarged by *compadrazgo*, the act of being a godparent for a baptized child. Taking on such a responsibility makes one part of the family. Hispanic sacramentality then has the potential to serve as a source of renewal for the Catholic family and larger community. To explore Hispanic sacramentality more deeply, take a statue of Our Lady of Guadalupe or a crucifix and visit your Hispanic parishioners. Ask what these images mean to them. Have a discussion and listen to their answers. Ask them about their families. Listen. What are they saying?

The Hispanic moment also can lead to more effective preaching. Hispanic culture is visual, and preachers can communicate more effectively by attending to visual elements such as stained-glass windows, crucifixes, art, while preaching. The early missionaries preached and catechized indigenous peoples with the help of these visual elements. Attention to the elements of good oral communication such as volume, pitch, pace, tone of voice, gestures, and eye contact, is another way that preaching to Latinos can be made more effective. Giving testimonies also is effective. Latinos (and all ethnicities) want to hear about how the Lord is alive and active both in the preacher's life and in the lives of the faithful. Consider setting up a preaching partner's group with Hispanic parishioners and meeting with them for two hours weekly between Monday and Friday. Ask them to tell you what they heard you say when you preached. You may want to have them fill out a preaching feedback form on the day you preach to them. This could include the central point of the homily, scriptural focus, and concrete examples. Spend the first half of this meeting reviewing their answers from the previous homily. Spend the second half of the meeting participating in *lectio divina* on the readings for the upcoming Sunday. Take notes on what they say to refer to in your homily preparation. This practice is a goldmine for your Sunday preaching.

The last contribution of the Hispanic moment for the U.S. Catholic Church is more foundational in that it concerns the Church at the level of her deepest identity. I maintain that the most important part of the Hispanic Moment is the development of an ecclesiology of communion to understand the Church. The Hispanic community is a real life, flesh and blood example of communion ecclesiology both in relationships and with respect to unity in diversity.

Communion ecclesiology focuses on relationships among the three persons of the Trinity, between human beings and God, among different human beings, and among the bishops and the pope. This focus on relationships takes flesh in the Hispanic community. Conversations often begin talking about family and health, not work or profession. The Hispanic family extends beyond the nuclear family to include grandparents, in-laws, nieces and nephews, and cousins. The Hispanic family is a microcosm of the Church in which relationships are primary and the good of the family supersedes the good of the individual. Individuals find their origin and fulfillment in the family, rather than as separate persons. Adopt two practices to grow in relationships with your Hispanic parishioners. First, begin to write the names of your Hispanic parishioners on three by five cards or on a smartphone using an App, such as Notes. Review these names every day. Try to connect names and faces. Second, begin to have a prayer list filled with the names of your Hispanic parishioners and what they asked you to pray for. Practicing these two disciplines and the assistance of the Holy Spirit can lead you to more pastoral charity for your Hispanic brothers and sisters.

The Hispanic community offers the U.S. Catholic Church a concrete manifestation of unity in diversity. This aspect of communion ecclesiology views diversity not as a threat but as an enrichment. The U.S. Catholic Church is the most diverse local church in the entire world, and the influx of Hispanic immigrants is a large part of this diversity. If fully embraced, a robust communion ecclesiology has the possibility to unite these new immigrants and their children in the bosom of the Church. List the various ethnicities of your parish. Set up an interview with members of each of those groups. Ask what blessings they bring to the local church. Ask how they can work for greater unity. Then invite all these interviewees together and have them share their answers to these questions. End the session with a time of prayer, interceding for greater unity in the Church. Offer one another the Sign of Peace and conclude with a final blessing.

Charity really is the most appropriate response to the Hispanic moment. Although elderly and with failing health, Deacon Bob served as deacon at our Hispanic Masses. He walked with a limp. He did not know the Spanish words for the parts of the Mass for the deacon, and knew only one word in Spanish: *gracias* (thank you). He said it often, pronouncing it with an English accent. Despite his language difficulties with Spanish, he spoke the most essential language: he spoke the language of love to our parishioners. When the Latinos would come to the sacristy, he always had time to listen to them, give them a hug, and say *gracias*. Instead of walking past Latino parishioners and not making eye contact, he shook every hand on the way to the back of the church before Mass. Charity is the most effective way to preach cross-culturally. Charity is indispensable.

Questions for Reflection and Discussion

1. Do you see any practices of popular religion in your parish? Is your parish fostering popular religion?

2. Do you notice Euro-American individualism in yourself or in your parish? What relationships are most important in your life and why?

3. How does the Hispanic understanding of signs and symbols have the potential to renew your parish and diocese?

4. Do you notice the diversity in your parish? Does it divide your community or unite it?

Conclusion

Immigration is changing countries and churches throughout the world. The Catholic Church in the U.S. is a local church, which is trying to respond to this enormous change. Developing preachers who can bridge the divide between cultures present in shared parishes is a critical goal for evangelization, catechesis, social justice, stewardship, and unity. Studying the past provides preachers with models of successful cross-cultural preaching. Considering the Hispanic moment and its particular gifts to the U.S. Catholic Church helps preachers be more aware of the present circumstances of ministry. These reflections help cross-cultural preachers to preach to various groups in shared parishes and thereby fulfill Jesus' command and desire that they may all become one.[1]

I conclude this preaching manual with an encouragement to cross-cultural preachers to foster two virtues: lifelong learning and humility. Cross-cultural preachers need to develop the habits of lifelong learning because trying to communicate to others from a different culture will always be challenging. This often involves learning a different language, such as Spanish or Vietnamese. Just as important, however, is the learning of culture. But this virtue of lifelong learning must be complemented by humility. Cross-cultural preachers can never say that they have arrived or achieved mastery of another culture. They should never become conceited or haughty but must constantly check their understanding of other cultures with natives of that culture. They always should be hesitant to speak with authority about a different culture. The cultivation of these two virtues, lifelong learning and humility, is a valuable contribution that cross-cultural preachers can make to the U.S. Catholic Church.

---

1 John 17:21.

Appendix

Sample Sermons in English and Spanish

A Homily for the Third Sunday in Advent (Year A)

In November 2015, an enormous amount of rain fell in a five-hour span on the Death Valley landscape in California. This unusual amount of rain caused a super bloom of wildflowers: a rare floral pageant of yellows, pinks, purples, and reds. The park ranger said, "When I first came to work here in the early 1990s, I kept hearing old timers talk about super blooms as a near mythical thing—the ultimate possibility of what a desert wildflower bloom could be. I never imagined that so much life could exist here in such staggering abundance and beauty."[1]

The prophet Isaiah describes a similar phenomenon in the Holy Land: "The desert and the parched land will exalt; the steppe will rejoice and bloom. They will bloom with abundant flowers, and rejoice with joyful song."[2] The cause of the flowers blooming in the desert was the end of the exile for the people of Israel. The people of Israel went into exile in 597 BC in Babylon. The prophet Isaiah maintains that the reason for the destruction of the Temple and the subsequent exile was the sin of the people. They were unfaithful to their covenant with God. Nevertheless, God remains faithful and does not abandon his people. Rather, he comes to help them, to deliver

---

[1] National Park Service, "Best Wildflower Bloom in a Decade," Feb. 19, 2016, https://www.nps.gov/deva/learn/news/wildlowers-2016.htm.

[2] Is 35:1–2.

them, and to return them to the Holy Land promised to Abraham and his descendants.

Today's Scripture is Isaiah's description of what this return will be like. It will be like a new Eden. Remember Eden was a verdant place, filled with plants and flowers and vegetation. Creation was good and uninfected by sin. Yet Adam and Eve, our first parents, chose to sin and disobey God, and this bad choice brought disorder to creation. Adam and Eve were banished from the garden of Eden. The return of the people from exile will be like a new Eden. Flowers will bloom in the desert and glorious vegetation will come forth from the dry land. Besides plants springing up from the earth, another sign of the return from exile will be physical healing: "Then will the eyes of the blind be opened, the ears of the deaf be cleared; then will the lame leap like a stag, then the tongue of the mute will sing."[3] And yet another sign will be praise and thanksgiving of the people: "Those whom the Lord has ransomed will return and enter Zion singing, crowned with everlasting joy; they will meet with joy and gladness, sorrow and mourning will flee."[4]

Let's move forward about 2000 years and talk about another decisive action of God in human history to change the course of history and to rescue a people. I direct your attention to the icon I have displayed of Saint Juan Diego to the right of the altar. On December 9th, 1531, Juan Diego was on his way to Mass early in the morning when he heard music coming from the top of a hill called Tepeyac. He also heard a voice saying: "Juanito, Juan Dieguito." There the Virgin Mary appeared to him and told him:

> Know and understand, you the dearest of my children, that I am the ever-holy Virgin Mary, Mother of the true God through whom one lives, of the Creator of heaven and of earth. I have a living desire that there be built a temple, so that in it I can show and give forth all my love, compassion, help, and defense, because I am your loving mother: to you, to all who are with you, to all the inhabitants of this land and to all who love me, call upon me, and trust in me, I will hear their lamentations and will remedy all their miseries, pains and sufferings. In order to bring about what my mercy intends, go to the palace of the bishop and tell him how I have sent you to manifest to him what I very much desire, that here on this site below the hill, a temple be built to me.[5]

Juan Diego does what the Virgin Mary says but has trouble convincing the bishop. After repeated visits to the bishop without success, the bishop

---

3 Is 35:5–6.

4 Is 35:10.

5 Virgilio Elizondo, *La Morenita: Evangelizer of the Americas* (San Antonio: Mexican American Cultural Center, 1980), 76.

asks Juan Diego to bring him a sign from the Blessed Virgin Mary. Juan Diego goes back to the hill of Tepeyac, and the Virgin appears to him again. She tells him to go to the top of the hill where he would find various flowers. She told him to cut and gather the flowers and bring them to her. He obeyed immediately and when he arrived at the top of Tepeyac, he was astounded to discover numerous exquisite roses from Castille, especially since it was long before their normal time. They had a beautiful aroma and were covered with the morning dew. He immediately began to cut them and returned to the Lady with the roses. She took them into her hands and rearranged them in his *tilma*. She then said:

> My son, the smallest of my children, this diversity of roses is the proof and sign that you will take to the bishop. You will tell him in my name that he is to see my will in this and he must fulfill it. You are my ambassador and most worthy of trust. I rigorously command you to unfold your mantle only in the presence of the bishop and to show him what you have with you. You are to tell everything. You will say that I told you to go to the top of the hill to cut the flowers, and tell everything that you saw and admired, so that you may convince the prelate to give his help in building the temple that I have asked for.[6]

Juan Diego takes the flowers in his *tilma*, and after much difficulty and opposition, is granted an audience with the bishop. He explains how the Virgin appeared to him again and what she said, and then unfolds his *tilma*. As all the roses dropped to the floor the precious image of the always holy Virgin Mary, Mother of God, appeared on the *tilma* in the presence of the bishop and his household. Immediately they fell to their knees amazed at this wonder of God.

Isn't God amazing and good? On Monday December 12, more than a thousand people will visit our parish church here and they will bring hundreds of flowers to offer to Our Lady of Guadalupe. This will be an amazing day for St. Mary's parish. Just like the first German immigrants at St. Mary's, they come to honor our Lady, to ask for her help, and to protect them and their loved ones. They ask for healing for their infirmities, peace and reconciliation in their marriages, help raising their children, aid in adjusting to the life of a new country, and steady employment to care for their families.

I encourage you to come to the church sometime this Monday December 12, and to see the flowers. The flowers are symbols of God's unexpected blessings in our lives. They are symbols of God's love and care for you. I would even go so far as encouraging you to buy some flowers and come to

---

6 Elizondo, 79.

the church and offer them to Mary Our Lady of Guadalupe and ask for God's favors in your life. Another option would be to buy some flowers for your home and spend some time thanking the Lord for the beauty of flowers. Or find images of flowers in magazines or on the Internet and spend some time looking at them. Or just imagine the most beautiful flowers you've ever seen in your lives. Use your imagination, but then conclude with praising and thanking God for the flowers.

Flowers represent God's unexpected blessings and favors shown to you. They increase our faith that God is with us, and they strengthen our hope. Advent is a time of hope for the Church. Hope means we look forward to the future and God's future blessings. Gazing upon the flowers and thanking God for them helps us to recall God's many blessings in our lives in the past, and now in the present, so that we may be filled with hope for the future. Take time this week to gaze upon the flowers and to give thanks and praise to God.

Una Homilía para el 3 Domingo de Adviento (año A)

En noviembre de 2015, una enorme cantidad de lluvia cayó en un lapso de cinco horas en el paisaje del Valle de la Muerte en California. Esta cantidad inusual de lluvia causó una súper floración de flores silvestres: un raro desfile floral de amarillos, rosas, púrpuras y rojos. El guardaparques dijo: "Cuando vine a trabajar aquí por primera vez a principios de la década de 1990, seguí escuchando a los veteranos hablar de las súper flores como algo casi mítico, la última posibilidad de lo que podría ser una floración de flores silvestres en el desierto. Nunca imaginé que tanta vida podría existir aquí en tan asombrosa abundancia y belleza."[7]

El profeta Isaías describe un fenómeno similar en la Tierra Santa:
"El desierto y la tierra reseca exaltarán; la estepa se regocijará y florecerá. Florecerán con abundantes flores y se regocijarán con canciones alegres."[8] La causa de las flores que florecían en el desierto fue el fin del exilio para el pueblo de Israel. El pueblo de Israel se exilió en 597 en Babilonia. El profeta Isaías sostiene que la razón de la destrucción del Templo y el posterior exilio fue el pecado del pueblo. Fueron infieles a su pacto con Dios. Sin embargo, Dios permanece fiel y no abandona a su pueblo. Más bien, viene a ayudarlos y liberarlos y devolverlos a la Tierra Santa, prometidos a Abraham y sus descendientes.

---

[7] National Park Service, "Best Wildflower Bloom in a Decade," Feb. 19, 2016, https://www.nps.gov/deva/learn/news/wildlowers-2016.htm (translated by author on April 29, 2022).

[8] Is 35:1–2.

La Escritura de hoy es la descripción de Isaías de cómo será este regreso. Será como un nuevo Edén. Recuerda que el Edén era un lugar verde, lleno de plantas, flores y vegetación. La creación era buena y no estaba infectada por el pecado. Sin embargo, Adán y Eva, nuestros primeros padres eligieron pecar y desobedecer a Dios, y esta mala elección trajo desorden a la creación. Adán y Eva fueron desterrados del jardín de Edén. El regreso del pueblo del exilio será como un nuevo Edén. Las flores florecerán en el desierto y la vegetación gloriosa surgirá de la tierra seca. Además de las plantas que brotan de la tierra, otro signo del regreso del exilio será la curación física: "Entonces se abrirán los ojos de los ciegos, se despejarán los oídos de los sordos; entonces saltará el cojo como un ciervo, luego cantará la lengua del mudo."[9] Otra señal será la alabanza y la acción de gracias del pueblo: "Los que el Señor ha rescatado volverán y entrarán en Sión cantando, coronados de gozo eterno; se encontrarán con alegría y alegría, la tristeza y el luto huirán."[10]

Avancemos unos 2000 años y hablemos de otra acción decisiva de Dios en la historia humana para cambiar el curso de la historia y rescatar a un pueblo. Dirijo su atención al icono que he mostrado de San Juan Diego a la derecha del altar. El nueve de diciembre de 1531 Juan Diego se dirigía a misa temprano en la mañana cuando escuchó música proveniente de la cima de un cerro llamado Tepeyac y escuchó una voz que decía: "Juanito, Juan Dieguito. Allí se le apareció la Virgen María y le dijo:

> Sabed y entend, vosotros, los más queridos de mis hijos, que yo soy la siempre santa Virgen María, Madre del verdadero Dios por el que se vive, del Creador del cielo y de la tierra. Tengo un deseo vivo de que se construya un templo, para que en él pueda mostrar y dar todo mi amor, compasión, ayuda y defensa, porque soy tu madre amorosa: a ti, a todos los que están contigo, a todos los habitantes de esta tierra y a todos los que me aman, invítame, y confía en mí, escucharé sus lamentaciones y remediaré todas sus miserias, dolores y sufrimientos. Para lograr lo que mi misericordia pretende, ve al palacio del obispo y dile cómo te he enviado a manifestarle lo que tanto deseo, que aquí, en este sitio debajo de la colina, se me construya un templo.[11]

Juan Diego hace lo que dice la virgen María, pero tiene problemas para convencer al Obispo. Después de repetidas visitas al Obispo y sin éxito, el Obispo le pide a Juan Diego que le traiga una señal de la Santísima Virgen

---

9 Is 35:5–6.

10 Is 35:10.

11 Virgilio Elizondo, *La Morenita: Evangelizer of the Americas* (San Antonio: Mexican American Cultural Center, 1980), 76 (translated by author).

María. Juan Diego vuelve al cerro del Tepeyac y la Virgen se le aparece de nuevo y le dice que vaya a la cima del cerro donde encontraría varias flores. Ella le dijo que cortara y recogiera las flores y se las trajera. Obedeció de inmediato y cuando llegó a la cima, se sorprendió al descubrir numerosas rosas exquisitas de Castilla, especialmente porque era mucho antes de su tiempo normal. Tenían un hermoso aroma y estaban cubiertos con el rocío de la mañana. Inmediatamente comenzó a cortarlos y regresó a la Señora con las rosas. Ella los tomó en sus manos y los reorganizó en su tilma. Luego dijo:

> Hijo mío, el más pequeño de mis hijos, esta diversidad de rosas es la prueba y la señal que llevarás al obispo. Le dirás en mi nombre que él debe ver mi voluntad en esto y que debe cumplirla. Usted es mi embajador y el más digno de confianza. Te ordeno rigurosamente que desprolijo tu manto sólo en presencia del obispo y que le muestres lo que tienes contigo. Debes contarlo todo. Dirás que te dije que fueras a la cima de la colina para cortar las flores, y contar todo lo que viste y admiraste, para que puedas convencer al prelado de que dé su ayuda en la construcción del templo que he pedido.[12]

Juan Diego toma las flores en su tilma, y después de mucha dificultad y oposición, se le concede una audiencia con el Obispo. Explica cómo la Virgen se le apareció de nuevo y lo que ella dijo, y luego despliega su tilma, y todas las rosas cayeron al suelo y como lo hicieron la preciosa imagen de la siempre santa virgen María, Madre de Dios, apareció en la tilma en presencia del obispo y su casa. Inmediatamente cayeron de rodillas asombrados por esta maravilla de Dios.

¿No es Dios asombroso y bueno? El lunes 12 de diciembre más de mil personas visitarán nuestra iglesia parroquial aquí y traerán cientos de flores para ofrecer a Nuestra Señora de Guadalupe. Este será un día increíble para la parroquia de la Asunción. Al igual que los primeros inmigrantes alemanes en asunción, vienen a honrar a Nuestra Señora y pedir su ayuda y protección para ellos y sus seres queridos. Piden curación para sus enfermedades, paz y reconciliación en sus matrimonios, ayuda para criar a sus hijos, ayuda para adaptarse a la vida de un nuevo país y empleo estable para cuidar a sus familias.

Te animo a que vengas a la iglesia en algún momento del lunes y a que veas las flores. Las flores son símbolos de las bendiciones inesperadas de Dios en nuestras vidas. Son símbolos del amor y cuidado de Dios por ti. Incluso iría tan lejos como para animarte a comprar algunas flores y venir a la iglesia y ofrecérselas a María Nuestra Señora de Guadalupe y pedir los favores de Dios en tu vida. Otra opción sería comprar algunas flores para su

---

[12] Elizondo, 79 (translated by author).

hogar y pasar algún tiempo agradeciendo al Señor por la belleza de las flores. Otra opción sería encontrar imágenes de flores en revistas o en Internet y pasar algunas mirándolas. Otra opción sería simplemente imaginar las flores más hermosas que hayas visto en tus vidas. Usa tu imaginación, pero luego concluye alabando y agradeciendo a Dios por las flores.

Las flores representan las bendiciones y favores inesperados de Dios que se te muestran. Aumentan nuestra fe en que Dios está con nosotros y fortalecen nuestra esperanza. El Adviento es un tiempo de esperanza para la Iglesia. Esperanza significa que esperamos el futuro y las bendiciones futuras de Dios. Contemplar las flores y agradecer a Dios por ellas ayuda a recordar las muchas bendiciones de Dios en nuestras vidas en el pasado, y ahora en el presente, para que podamos estar llenos de esperanza para el futuro. Tómese el tiempo esta semana para contemplar las flores y dar gracias y alabanza a Dios.

A Homily for the 24th Sunday in Ordinary Time: Year B

How many have a vocation here? Raise your hands. Vocation comes from *vocare*—which is Latin for to call. That's where we get the words vocabulary, vocal, vociferous. When you think of vocation, you may think of a vocation to religious life, or priesthood. But vocation means calling. It means a calling from God. Do you think that God continues to speak to us and to call us? Then we all have vocations because we are all called by God in big ways and in little ways.[13]

Did Jesus have a vocation? You bet he did. He was fully human like us in all things but sin. He too had to pray and study and reflect upon the Scriptures to find his vocation. Jesus studied the Law and the prophets and there he found the inspired word of Yahweh speaking to him: "the Lord God opens my ear that I may hear; and I have not rebelled, have not turned back."[14] Jesus read and meditated upon this mysterious suffering servant who "gave his back to those who beat him, and his cheeks to those who plucked his beard."[15] Jesus heard his Abba, his Father, through these words from the

---

[13] Please see Chapter 7, which speaks about six ways that Hispanic preaching expresses sacramentality. The last is preaching as performance. I highlight the similarities between Black preaching and preaching to Latinos. Both involve call and response. The beginning of this homily is filled with call and response: I invite the congregation to respond by asking good questions and listening to their answers.

[14] Is 50:5.

[15] Is 50:6.

prophet Isaiah. He was able to connect these words to the words spoken to him in prayer by his Abba, his Father.[16]

Jesus reveals his vocation to his disciples: "He began to teach them that the Son of Man must suffer greatly and be rejected by the elders, the chief priests, and the scribes, and be killed, and rise after three days."[17] When did Jesus come to this understanding of his vocation? How did he do it? He probably spent nights in prayer speaking and listening to Abba, his Father. Only through a daily life of prayer did he come to this understanding, this calling.

How did his disciples receive it? For Peter it was like scratching your fingernails on a chalkboard. Although Peter calls him the Christ, the true king of Israel, he doesn't envision the true king going to a shameful death. He has his own ideas of the Christ and Jesus' future Passion, Death, and Resurrection are not part of his ideas, his plans. That's why Jesus rebukes him so sharply: "Get behind me, Satan. You are thinking not as God does, but as human beings do."[18] Jesus has heard his Abba, his Father calling him to this path of the Cross and Resurrection, and Satan opposes it. This is the way God has determined to defeat evil in a definitive way, and Satan and Peter oppose him.

In rebuking Peter, Jesus looks at his disciples. He uses this as a teaching moment. He's looking at us too. He says, "Whoever wishes to come after me must deny himself, pick up his cross, and follow me. For whoever wishes to save his life will lose it, but whoever loses his life for my sake and that of the gospel will save it."[19] Thomas More in the play *A Man for All Seasons* opposes the king's desire to divorce his wife so that he can marry Anne Boleyn. He refuses to take the oath to the king. Richard Rich opposes him and betrays him in court so that he can take ownership of Wales, a backwater area of England. In a dramatic scene, Thomas More says, "Why, Richard, it profits a man nothing to give his soul for the whole world.... But for Wales!"[20] Thomas More goes to his death a faithful disciple of Jesus Christ and the Catholic Church, whereas Richard betrays the Lord, the Church, and Thomas More, for Wales.

---

[16] A second way this homily was good for preaching to Latinos is its oral nature. I preached a homily without notes and manuscript and had a heart-to-heart conversation with the congregation. I had one theme and developed this theme through an admittedly cross-cultural example of Thomas More. This is an illustration of the theme that allows the Hispanics to see it in their mind's eye.

[17] Mk 8:31.

[18] Mk 8:33.

[19] Mk 8:34–35.

[20] Robert Bolt, *A Man for All Seasons: A Play in Two Acts* (London: Heinemann, 1960), 95.

What is our response to the call who do you say that I am? Like Jesus, who heard his Abba, his Father calling him, Jesus is calling us to be his faithful disciples by renouncing ourselves, picking up our crosses and following him. Pope Francis is calling all Catholics to listen to the voice of the Lord calling them to follow him. The Holy Father wants all of us to hear the call to become a faithful disciple and to respond this call generously. That's what the pope means when he talks about an encounter with the Lord. This renewed encounter is central to his desire to renew the church.

The call the Lord issues to us through Pope Francis has occurred in the life of the Church for 2000 years. In the fifth century, St. Benedict called men to become monks and he said, "Let us ... attentively hear the Divine Voice, calling and exhorting us daily: 'Today if you shall hear his voice, harden not your hearts'" (Ps. 95:7–8; Prologue of the Rule of St. Benedict).[21] In the thirteenth century St. Francis helped people respond to the Lord's call to follow him. In the fifteenth and sixteenth centuries, St. Ignatius helped men who later became Jesuits to respond to this call from the Lord. Today Pope Francis is calling all Catholics to embrace this calling as their own.[22]

This call is a call to know Jesus more in his Passion, Death, and Resurrection and to follow him more faithfully in our daily lives. As we celebrate this Eucharist, we enter into this mystery in a deeper way. Be attentive to the words and actions and the mystery we celebrate at the altar. Let what is happening lead to a new encounter with the Lord who loves you so much that he calls you personally to follow him.

24° Domingo del Tiempo Ordinario: Año B

¿Cuántos oyentes tienen una vocación aquí? Levanta las manos. La vocación viene de *vocare*, que en latín significa llamar. Ahí es donde obtenemos las palabras vocabulario, vocal, vociferante, etc. ... Cuando piensas en la vocación, puedes pensar en una vocación a la vida religiosa, o al sacerdocio. Pero vocación significa un llamado de Dios. ¿Crees que Dios continúa hablándonos y llamándonos? Entonces todos tenemos vocaciones porque todos somos llamados por Dios en grandes y pequeñas maneras.

¿Tuvo Jesús una vocación? ¡Claro que si! Él era completamente humano como nosotros en todas las cosas excepto en el pecado. Él también tuvo que orar, estudiar y reflexionar sobre las Escrituras para encontrar su vocación.

---

[21] St. Benedict, *The Rule of St. Benedict*, trans. By Anthony Meisel and M.L. del Mastro (New York: Doubleday, 1975), 43.

[22] Another way this homily is good cross-cultural communication to Latinos is testimony. I focus on having an encounter with Jesus. Pope Francis calls the whole church to have this encounter. And I extend this call to the Latino community in this example of cross-cultural preaching.

Jesús estudiaba la Ley y los profetas y allí encontraba la palabra inspirada de Yahvé hablándole: "el Señor Dios abre mi oído para que pueda oír; y no me he rebelado, no he dado marcha atrás".[23] Jesús leyó y meditó sobre este misterioso siervo sufriente que dio "... su espalda a los que lo golpearon, y sus mejillas a los que le arrancaron la barba".[24] Jesús escuchó a su Abba, su Padre, a través de estas palabras de Isaías. Él fue capaz de conectar estas palabras del profeta Isaías con las palabras que le dijo en oración su Abba, su Padre.

Jesús revela su vocación a sus discípulos: "Comenzó a enseñarles que el Hijo del Hombre debe sufrir mucho y ser rechazado por los ancianos, los principales sacerdotes y los escribas, y ser asesinado, y resucitar después de tres días".[25] ¿Cuándo llegó Jesús a este entendimiento de su vocación? ¿Cómo lo hizo? Probablemente pasaba noches en oración hablando y escuchando a Abba, su Padre. Sólo a través de una vida diaria de oración llegaba a este entendimiento, a este llamado.

¿Cómo lo recibieron sus discípulos? Para Pedro era como rascarse las uñas en una pizarra. Aunque Pedro lo llama el Cristo, el verdadero rey de Israel, no imagina que el verdadero rey vaya a una muerte vergonzosa. Él tiene sus propias ideas de Cristo y la futura pasión, muerte y resurrección de Jesús no son parte de sus ideas, sus planes. Es por eso por lo que Jesús lo reprende tan bruscamente: "Ponte detrás de mí, Satanás. No estás pensando como Dios lo hace, sino como lo hacen los seres humanos".[26] Jesús ha escuchado a su Abba, su Padre llamándolo a este camino de la cruz y la resurrección y Satanás se opone a él. Esta es la forma en que Dios ha determinado derrotar al mal de una manera definitiva, y Satanás y Pedro se oponen a él.

Al reprender a Pedro, Jesús mira a sus discípulos. Él usa esto como un momento de enseñanza. Él también nos está mirando. Él dice: "Si alguien quiere seguirme, debe renunciar a sí mismo, tomar su cruz y seguirme. Los que salvan sus vidas los perderán, los que pierden sus vidas por mi causa y el evangelio los salvará".[27] Thomas More en la obra *A Man for All Seasons* se opone al deseo del Rey de divorciarse de su esposa para poder casarse con Anne Boleyn. Se niega a prestar juramento al Rey. Richard Rich se opone a él y lo traiciona en la corte para que pueda tomar posesión de Gales, un área remansada de Inglaterra. En una escena dramática, Thomas More le dice: "Richard, nunca le beneficia a un hombre ganar el mundo entero y perder

---

23 Is 50:5.
24 Is 50:6.
25 Marcos 8:31.
26 Marcos 8:33.
27 Marcos 8:34–35.

su alma. ¿Pero para Gales, Richard, pero para Gales?"[28] Thomas More va a su muerte como un fiel discípulo de Jesucristo y de la Iglesia Católica, mientras que Richard traiciona al Señor, a la Iglesia, y a Thomas More, por Gales.

¿Cuál es nuestra respuesta al llamado ¿quién dices que soy? Como Jesús, que escuchó a su Abba, su Padre llamándolo, Jesús nos está llamando a ser sus fieles discípulos renunciando a nosotros mismos, recogiendo nuestras cruces y siguiéndolo. El Papa Francisco está llamando a todos los católicos a escuchar la voz del Señor llamándolos a seguirlo. El santo Padre quiere que todos escuchemos la llamada a convertirnos en discípulos fieles y respondamos generosamente a esta llamada. Eso quiere decir el Papa cuando habla de un Encuentro con el Señor. Este encuentro renovado es central para su deseo de renovar la iglesia.

La llamada que el Señor nos hace a través del Papa Francisco ha ocurrido en la vida de la Iglesia durante 2000 años. En el siglo V, San Benito llamó a los hombres a convertirse en monjes y dijo: "Escuchemos atentamente la Voz Divina, llamándonos y exhortándonos diariamente: 'Hoy, si oís su voz, no endurezcáis vuestros corazones'" (Sal. 95:7–8; Prólogo de la Regla de San Benito).[29] En el siglo 13 San Francisco ayudó a la gente a responder al llamado del Señor a seguirlo. En los siglos 15 y 16 San Ignacio les ayudó a hombres a responder a este llamado del Señor. Hoy el Papa Francisco está llamando a todos los católicos, a todos los cristianos a escuchar este llamado del Señor.

Este llamado es un llamado a conocer más a Jesús en su pasión, muerte y resurrección y a seguirlo más fielmente en nuestra vida diaria. Al celebrar esta Eucaristía, entramos en este Misterio de una manera más profunda. Estad atentos a las palabras y acciones y al misterio que celebramos en el altar. Deja que lo que está sucediendo te lleve a un nuevo Encuentro con el Señor que te ama tanto que te llama personalmente a seguirlo.

---

28 Robert Bolt, *A Man for All Seasons: A Play in Two Acts* (London: Heinemann, 1960), 95 (translated into Spanish by author).

29 St. Benedict, *The Rule of St. Benedict*, trans. By Anthony Meisel and M.L. del Mastro (New York: Doubleday, 1975), 43 (translated into Spanish by author).

Bibliography

Alvarez, Victor. "Preaching to Generation X." In *Preaching and Culture in Latino Congregations*, edited by Kenneth Davis and Jorge Presmanes, 120–39. Chicago: Liturgy Training Publications, 2000.

Baker, Kimberly. "Proclaiming a Dynamic Understanding of Grace: The Spiritual Foundation for Sacramental and Liturgical Catechesis," *Worship* 89, no. 6 (Nov. 2015): 506–25. Accessed Sept. 3, 2017. ATLASerials, Religion Collection, EBSCOhost.

Benedict XVI. *Sacramentum Caritatis*. Apostolic Exhortation. February 22, 2007. Accessed June 26, 2017. http://w2.vatican.va/content/benedict-xvi/en/apost_exhortations/documents/hf_ben-xvi_exh_20070222_sacramentum-caritatis.html.

———. *Verbum Domini*. Apostolic Exhortation. September 30, 2010. Accessed June 26, 2017. http://w2.vatican.va/content/benedict-xvi/en/apost_exhortations/documents/hf_ben-xvi_exh_20100930_verbum-domini.html.

Bevans, Stephen, ed. *Mission & Culture: The Louis J. Luzbetak Lectures*. Maryknoll, NY: Orbis Books, 2012.

Carter Florence, Anna. *Preaching as Testimony*. Louisville: Westminster John Knox Press, 2007.

Catechism of the Catholic Church: Revised in Accordance with the Official Latin Text Promulgated by Pope John Paul II. 2nd ed. Vatican City: Liberia Editrice Vaticana, 1997.

Cavadini, John. "Preaching and Catechesis: Mending the Rift between Scripture and Doctrine." In *We Preach Christ Crucified*, edited by Michael Connors, 66–82. Collegeville, MN: Liturgical Press, 2014.

Centers for Disease Control and Prevention (CDC). "About Teen Pregnancy." November 15, 2021. https://www.cdc.gov/teenpregnancy/about/index.htm.

Childers, Jana, and Clayton Schmit, eds. *Performance in Preaching: Bringing the Sermon to Life*. Grand Rapids: Baker Academic, 2008.

Christian, William. "Spain in Latino Religiosity." In *El Cuerpo de Cristo: The Hispanic Presence in the U.S. Catholic Church*, ed. Peter Casarella and Raul Gomez. New York: Crossroad, 1998.

Clooney, Francis. "Roberto de Nobili, Adaptation and the Reasonable Interpretation of Religion." *Missiology: An International Review* 18, no. 1 (January 1990): 25–36.

Congregation for the Clergy. *General Directory for Catechesis*. Washington, DC: United States Catholic Conference, 1998.

Congregation for Divine Worship and Discipline of the Sacraments. *Homiletic Directory*. Vatican City: Libreria Editrice Vaticana, 2014. Accessed June 26, 2017. http://www.vatican.va/roman_curia/congregations/ccdds/documents/rc_con_ccdds_doc_20140629_direttorio-omiletico_en.html

Connors, Michael, and Ann Garrido, "Doctrinal and Catechetical Preaching," In *A Catholic Handbook for Preaching*, edited by Edward Foley, Catherine Vincie, and Richard Fragomeni, 124–33. Collegeville, MN: Liturgical Press, 2016.

Cox, Richard. *Rewiring Your Preaching: How the Brain Processes Sermons*. Downers Grove, IL: IVP Books, 2012.

Davis, Kenneth, ed. *Misa, Mesa, y Musa: Liturgy in the U.S. Hispanic Church*. Schiller Park, IL: World Library Publications, 1997.

Davis, Kenneth, and Leopoldo Perez, eds. *Preaching the Teaching: Hispanics, Homiletics, and Catholic Social Justice Doctrine*. Chicago: University of Scranton Press, 2005.

———. "Hispanic Catholics Deserve More from Their Church." *U.S. Catholic* 73 (February 2008): 24–26.

———. "Becoming a Cross-Cultural Preacher." In *We Preach Christ Crucified*, edited by Michael Connors, 167–80. Collegeville, MN: Liturgical Press, 2014.

Davis, Kenneth, and Jorge Presmanes, eds. *Preaching and Culture in Latino Congregations*. Chicago: Liturgy Training Publications, 2000.

DeBona, Guerric. "Preaching after Vatican II." In *A Catholic Handbook for Preaching*, edited by Edward Foley, Catherine Vincie, and Richard Fragomeni, 96–97. Collegeville, MN: Liturgical Press, 2016.

Deck, Allan Figueroa. "Evangelization as Conceptual Framework for the Church's Mission: The Case of U.S. Hispanics." In *Evangelizing America*, edited by Thomas Rausch, 85–110. New York: Paulist Press, 2004.

———. "A Latino Practical Theology: Mapping the Road Ahead." *Theological Studies* 65, no. 2 (November 2004): 275–97.

———. "Where the Laity Flourish." *America* 195 (August 14–21, 2006): 14–16.

———. "Hispanic Ministry: New Realities and Choices. *Origins* 38 (December 4, 2008): 405–11.

Deck, Allan Figueroa, Virgilio Elizondo, and Timothy Matovina, eds. *The Treasure of Guadalupe*. Lanham, MD: Rowman & Littlefield, 2006.

DeLeers, Stephen. *Written Text Becomes Living Word: The Vision and Practice of Sunday Preaching*. Collegeville, MN: Liturgical Press, 2004.

Dulles, Avery. *Models of the Church*. New York: Doubleday, 1987.

———. "Vatican II on the Interpretation of Scripture." *Letter and Spirit* 2 (2006): 17–26.

Earley, Christopher, and Soon Ang. *Cultural Intelligence: Individual Interactions across Cultures*. Stanford, CA: Stanford University Press, 2003.

Edwards, O. C. *A History of Preaching*. Nashville: Abingdon Press, 2004.

Elizondo, Virgilio. "Our Lady of Guadalupe as a Cultural Symbol." In *Mestizo Worship: A Pastoral Approach to Liturgical Ministry*, edited by Virgilio Elizondo and Timothy Matovina, 37–47. Collegeville, MN: Liturgical Press, 1998.

———. *The Future is Mestizo: Life Where Cultures Meet*. Denver: University Press of Colorado, 2000.

———. *Galilean Journey: The Mexican-American Promise*. New York: Orbis Books, 2003.

———. *A God of Incredible Surprises: Jesus of Galilee*. Lanham, MD: Rowman & Littlefield, 2003.

———. "Jesus the Galilean Jew in Mestizo Theology." *Theological Studies* 70 (2009): 262–80.

Empereur, James and Eduardo Fernandez. *La Vida Sacra: Contemporary Hispanic Sacramental Theology*. Lanham, MD: Rowman & Littlefield Publishers, 2006.

Espin, Orlando. *Building Bridges, Doing Justice: Constructing a Latino/a Ecumenical Theology*. Maryknoll, NY: Orbis Books, 2009.

Extraordinary Synod of Bishops 1985. *Final Report* II B a, 4. Available online at www.ewtn.com/catholicism/library/final-report-of-the-1985-extraordinary-synod-2561.

Farey, Caroline, Waltraud Linnig, and Johannah Paruch, eds. *The Pedagogy of God: Its Centrality in Catechesis and Catechist Formation*. Steubenville, OH: Emmaus Road Publishing, 2011.

Fernandez, Eduardo. *La Cosecha: Harvesting Contemporary United States Hispanic Theology (1972–1998)*. Collegeville, MN: Liturgical Press, 2000.

———. *Mexican-American Catholics*. Mahwah, NJ: Paulist Press, 2007.

Flores, Nicole. "Latina/o Families: Solidarity and the Common Good." *Journal of the Society of Christian Ethics* 33, no. 2 (2013): 57–72.

Foley, Con, and Richard Fragomeni. "Roman Catholic Teaching on Preaching: A Postconciliar Survey." In *A Catholic Handbook for Preaching*, edited by Edward Foley, Catherine Vincie, and Richard Fragomeni, 26–38. Collegeville, MN: Liturgical Press, 2016.

Foley, Edward. "The Homily." In *A Catholic Handbook for Preaching*, edited by Edward Foley, Catherine Vincie, and Richard Fragomeni, 156–65. Collegeville, MN: Liturgical Press, 2016.

Francis. *Evangelii Gaudium*. Apostolic Exhortation. November 24, 2013. Accessed June 26, 2017. http://w2.vatican.va/content/francesco/en/apost_exhortations/documents/papa-francesco_esortazione-ap_20131124_evangelii-gaudium.html.

Francis, Mark. *Local Worship, Global Church: Popular Religion and the Liturgy*. Collegeville, MN: Liturgical Press, 2014.

———. "Liturgy and Inculturation since Vatican II: Where Are We? What Have We Learned?" *Worship* 91 (January 2017): 24–42.

Garcia, Sixto, and Orlando Espin. "Lilies of the Field: A Hispanic Theology of Providence and Human Responsibility." *Proceedings of the Catholic Theological Society of America* 44 (1989): 70–90.

Gautier, Mary. *Catholic Ministry Formation Enrollments: Statistical Overview for 2008–2009.* Washington, DC: Center for Applied Research in the Apostolate, 2009.

Goizueta, Roberto. *Caminemos con Jesus: Toward a Hispanic/Latino Theology of Accompaniment.* Maryknoll, NY: Orbis Books, 1995.

———. "Fiesta: Life in the Subjunctive," in *From the Heart of our People*, edited by Orlando Espin and Miguel Diaz, 84–99. Maryknoll, NY: Orbis Books, 1999.

———. *Christ Our Companion: Toward a Theological Aesthetics of Liberation.* Maryknoll, New York: Orbis, 2009.

Gomez, Raul. "Preaching the Ritual Masses among Latinos." In *Preaching and Culture in Latino Congregations,* edited by Kenneth Davis and Jorge Presmanes, 103–19. Chicago: Liturgy Training Publications, 2000.

Gonzales, Justo. "Welcoming the Stranger." *Apuntes* 35, no. 3 (2015): 90–97.

———. "Reading the Bible from the Edges of Society." *Apuntes* 35, no. 2 (2015): 38–53.

González, Justo, and Catherine González. "Preaching that Welcomes the Stranger." *Journal for Preachers* 32, no. 4 (2009): 18–22.

———. "Preaching Pentecost in Today's Changing World." *Journal for Preachers* 35, no. 4 (2012): 15–20.

González, Justo, and Pablo Jiménez. *Púlpito: An Introduction to Hispanic Preaching.* Nashville: Abingdon Press, 2005.

Groome, Thomas. "A Shared Praxis Model for Bible Study." *Review and Expositor* 107 (Spring, 2010): 177–96.

———. *Will There Be Faith? A New Vision for Educating and Growing Disciples.* New York: HarperCollins, 2011.

Hoover, Brett. *The Shared Parish: Latinos, Anglos, and the Future of U.S. Catholicism.* New York: New York University Press, 2014.

Huebsch, Bill. *Handbook for Success in Whole Community Catechesis.* Mystic, CT: Twenty-Third Publications, 2004.

Hughes, Kathleen. *Becoming the Sign: Sacramental Living in a Post-Conciliar Church.* New York: Paulist Press, 2013.

Irwin, Kevin. "A Sacramental World—Sacramentality as the Primary Language of the Sacraments." *Worship* 76 (May 2002): 197–211.

John Paul II. *Catechesi Tradendae.* Apostolic Exhortation. October 16, 1979. Accessed June 26, 2017. http://w2.vatican.va/content/john-paul-ii/en/apost_exhortations/documents/hf_jp-ii_exh_16101979_catechesi-tradendae.html.

———. *Redemptoris Missio*. Encyclical Letter. December 7, 1990. Accessed June 26, 2017. http://w2.vatican.va/content/john-paul-ii/en/encyclicals/documents/hf_jpii_enc_07121990_redemptoris-missio.html.

———. *Fidei Depositum*. Apostolic Constitution, October 11, 1992.

———. Address to the Pontifical Biblical Commission. *The Interpretation of the Bible in the Church*. Boston: St. Paul Books and Media, 1993.

Johnson-Mondragon, Ken, ed. *Pathways of Hope and Faith among Hispanic Teens: Pastoral Reflections and Strategies Inspired by the National Study of Youth and Religion*. Stockton, CA: Instituto Fe y Vida, 2007.

Kim, Matthew. *Preaching and Cultural Intelligence: Understanding the People Who Hear Our Sermons*. Grand Rapids: Baker Academic, 2017.

Lara, Jaime. "Visual Preaching: The Witness of Our Latin Eyes." In *Preaching and Culture in Latino Congregations*, edited by Kenneth Davis and Jorge Presmanes, 75–92. Chicago: Liturgy Training Publications, 2000.

Levada, William. "The Homilist: Teacher of Faith." *Origins* 37, no. 38 (2008): 605.

The Liturgy Documents: A Parish Resource, 3rd ed. Chicago: Liturgy Training Publications, 1991.

Lorance, Cody. "Cultural Relevance and Doctrinal Soundness: The Mission of Roberto de Nobili." *Missiology: An International Review* 33, no. 4 (October 2005): 415–24.

Matovina, Timothy. "No Melting Pot in Sight." In *Perspectivas: Hispanic Ministry*, edited by Deck, Tarango, and Matovina, 35–39. Kansas City: Sheed & Ward, 1995.

———. *Latino Catholicism: Transformation in America's Largest Church*. Princeton: Princeton University Press, 2012.

Miranda, Ida. "Faith Formation with Hispanic/Latino Families." *Lifelong Faith* (Summer 2007): 1–9.

Nanko-Fernandez, Carmen. "From *Pájaro* to Paraclete: Retrieving the Spirit of God in the Company of Mary." In *Building Bridges, Doing Justice: Constructing a Latino/a Ecumenical Theology*, edited by Orlando Espin, 13–28. Maryknoll, NY: Orbis Books, 2009.

National Conference of Catholic Bishops, Bishops' Committee on Priestly Life and Ministry. *Fulfilled in Your Hearing: The Homily in the Sunday Assembly*. Washington, DC: United States Catholic Conference, 1982.

———. *Encuentro & Mission: A Renewed Pastoral Framework for Hispanic Ministry*. Washington, DC: United States Catholic Conference, 2002.

———. *National Directory for Catechesis*. Washington, DC: United States Conference of Catholic Bishops, 2005.

———. *Best Practices for Shared Parishes: So That They May All Be One*. Washington, DC: United States Conference of Catholic Bishops, 2014.

Negrete, Jorge. *Mexico lindo y querido*, Found on Letras.com, accessed January 10, 2020, https://www.letras.com/jorge-negrete/894891/

New Commentary on the Code of Canon Law, edited by John Beal, James Coriden, and Thomas Green. Mahwah, NJ: Paulist Press, 2000.

Nieman, James, and Thomas Rogers. *Preaching to Every Pew: Cross-Cultural Strategies*. Minneapolis: Augsburg Fortress Press, 2001.

O'Malley, John. *What Happened at Vatican II*. Cambridge, MA.: Belknap Press, 2010.

O'Meara, Thomas. *Theology of Ministry*. New York: Paulist Press, 1999.

Ospino, Hosffman. "Foundations for an Intercultural Philosophy of Christian Education." *Religious Education* 104, no. 3 (May–June 2009).

———. "Hispanic Ministry, Faith Formation, and Evangelization." In *Hispanic Ministry Present and Future*, edited by Hosffman Ospino. Miami: Convivium Press, 2010.

———. "Theological Horizons for a Pedagogy of Accompaniment." *Religious Education* 105, no. 4 (July-September 2010): 413–29.

———. "Catechesis, Diversity, and Culture: The Importance of (Re)Definitions." *New Theology Review* 24, no. 1 (February 2011): 5–19.

———. *Evangelización y catequesis in el ministerio hispano: Guia para la formación en la fe*. Liguori, MO: Liguori Press, 2013.

———. "Religious Education and the Communal Shaping of a Christian Social Consciousness: The Testimony of Cesar Chavez." *Religious Education* 108, no. 4 (July-September 2013): 403–17.

———. *Hispanic Ministry in Catholic Parishes: A Summary Report of Findings from the National Study of Catholic Parishes with Hispanic Ministry*. Boston: Boston College, 2014. Accessed April 11, 2017.

———. *Interculturalism and Catechesis: A Catechist's Guide to Responding to Cultural Diversity*. New London, CT: Twenty-Third Publications, 2017.

Paul VI. *Mysterium Fidei*. Encyclical Letter, September 3, 1965. Accessed June 26, 2017. http://w2.vatican.va/content/paul-vi/en/encyclicals/documents/hf_p-vi_enc_03091965_mysterium.html.

———. *Evangelii Nuntiandi*. Apostolic Exhortation, December 8, 1975. Accessed June 26, 2017. http://w2.vatican.va/content/paul-vi/en/apost_exhortations/documents/hf_p-vi_exh_19751208_evangelii-nuntiandi.html.

Pauley, James. *Liturgical Catechesis in the 21st Century: A School of Discipleship*. Chicago: Liturgy Training Publications, 2017.

Pecklers, Keith. Worship: *A Primer in Christian Ritual*. Collegeville, MN: Liturgical Press, 2005.

Presmanes, Jorge. "The Juxtaposition of Dangerous Memories: Toward a Latino Theology of Preaching from the Underside of the Diaspora Experience." In *Preaching and Culture in Latino Congregations,* edited by Kenneth Davis and Jorge Presmanes, 5–26. Chicago: Liturgy Training Publications, 2000.

———. "Bilingual Liturgy: A U.S. Latino Perspective." *Liturgical Ministry* 16 (Summer 2007): 139–46.

Presmanes, Jorge, and Alicia Marill. "Hispanic Ministry and Theology." In *Hispanic Ministry*, edited by Hosffman Ospino, 81–97. Miami: Convivium Press, 2013.

Pius XII. *Mediator Dei*. Encyclical Letter, November 20, 1947. Accessed June 26, 2017. http://w2.vatican.va/content/pius-xii/en/encyclicals/documents/hf_p-xii_enc_20111947_mediator-dei.html.

Raj, Victor. "Text and Context in Indian Christian Theology." *Missio Apostolica* 16, no. 2 (Nov. 2008):115.

Sacred Congregation for Bishops. *Ecclesiae Imago* [Directory on the Pastoral Ministry of Bishops, 1973]. Ottawa: Canadian Catholic Conference Publications Service, 1973.

Sensing, Tim. *Qualitative Research: A Multi-Methods Approach to Projects for Doctor of Ministry Thesis*. Eugene, OR: Wipf and Stock Publishers, 2011.

Smith, Christian, and Kari Christofferson, Hilary Davidson, and Patricia Snell Herzog. *Lost in Transition: The Dark Side of Emerging Adulthood*. New York: Oxford University Press, 2011.

Smith, Christian, and Melinda Denton. *Soul Searching: The Religious and Spiritual Lives of American Teenagers*. New York: Oxford University Press, 2005.

Smith, Christian, Kyle Longest, Jonathan Hill, and Kari Christofferson. *Young Catholic America: Emerging Adults In, Out of, and Gone From the Church*. New York: Oxford University Press, 2014.

Smith, Christian, and Patricia Snell. *Souls in Transition: The Religious & Spiritual Lives of Emerging Adults*. New York: Oxford University Press, 2009.

St. Mary's Press & CARA. *Going, Going, Gone: The Dynamics of Disaffiliation in Young Catholics*. Winona, MN: St. Mary's Press, 2017.

Tanner, Norman P., *Decrees of the Ecumenical Councils*. 2 vols. Washington, DC: Georgetown University Press, 1990.

Tubbs Tisdale, Leonora. *Preaching as Local Theology and Folk Art*. Minneapolis: Augsburg Fortress Press, 1997.

United States Conference of Catholic Bishops. *Best Practices for Shared Parishes: So That They May All Be One*. Washington, DC: United States Conference of Catholic Bishops, 2014.

———. *V National Encuentro of Hispanic/Latino Ministry: Missionary Disciples: Witnesses of God's Love; Working Document*. Washington, DC: USCCB, 2018.

Vatican Council II. *Ad Gentes*. Decree on Missionary Activity of the Church, December 7, 1965. In *Vatican Council II: The Conciliar and Post Conciliar Documents*, edited by Austin Flannery. Northport, NY: Costello Publishing Company, 1996.

———. *Gaudium et Spes*. Constitution on the Church and the World of Today, December 7, 1965. In *Vatican Council II*, edited by Flannery.

Waznak, Robert. *An Introduction to the Homily*. Collegeville, MN: Liturgical Press, 1998.

Weddell, Sherry. *Forming Intentional Disciples: The Path to Knowing and Following Jesus.* Huntington, IN: Our Sunday Visitor, 2012.

White, Joseph. *The Way God Teaches: Catechesis and the Divine Pedagogy.* Huntington, IN: Our Sunday Visitor, 2014.

Wright, N. T. *The New Testament and the People of God.* Volume 1 of *Christian Origins and the Question of God.* Minneapolis: Fortress Press, 1992.

Zech, Charles et al. *Catholic Parishes of the 21st Century.* New York: Oxford University Press, 2017.

Index

A *abuelas* (grandmothers), 42, 101
accommodatio, 7–9
Advent, 32, 97–98, 109–15
anointing of the sick, 21, 88
archangels, 94–95
Argentina, 94
arras (coins), 84–85
Aztecs, 47, 84

B Baptism, 62, 67, 70–73, 80, 85
blessings: of the sick, 88; of unborn and newborn babies, 70; of workers and tools, 96
burial, 90–91

C caste system, 6–8
catechesis. *See* faith formation
catechesis familiar (family catechesis), 74–75, 77
cemetery, 90–91
Chaput, Charles (Archbishop), 12
children: blessings of unborn and newborn babies, 70; and difficulties in Latino families, 34; drawing parents to God and the Church, 83–84; hearing confessions of, 87; preaching to, 75–80; and sacramental preparation, 70–81

Christian, William, 49
Church, theology of, 24–28, 104–5
clergy: and noninstitutional nature of Hispanic popular religion, 41–42, 52–54, 102–3; readiness for Hispanic moment, 21–22, 28; seminary formation for Latino ministry, xii, 14, 18, 21–22
Columbus, Christopher, 47, 48
communion ecclesiology, 24–28, 104–5
compadrazgo (institution of godparents), 73, 103. *See also* godparents
confession: by children, 87; of family sins, 27, 76, 86, 87; first Reconciliation, 74, 76–77, 83; frequently received by Hispanic Catholics, 77, 86; by women, 86, 87–88
Confirmation, 77–79
Congregation for the Doctrine of the Faith (CDF), 26
Connors, Michael, 3
Conquista (conquest), 31, 47, 48, 49
Covid-19, 34, 88
creation, 50–51
creed, 3
Cristo Rey (Christ the King), 97

D death, 21–22, 88–91
día de los muertos (Day of the Dead), 89, 91
dichos (adages or aphorisms), 58, 64
Dulles, Avery, 53

E Ecuador, 95f, 97
El Salvador, 96–97
Empereur, James, 25nn6–7, 37n2, 41n9, 41n11, 48nn3–4, 57, 74nn4–6
Encuentro, 12, 17–18, 81
Espin, Orlando, 42
Eucharist: first Communion, 75–76, 83; and Hispanic popular religion, 43, 44–45, 102; theology of, 62, 63, 85
evangelization: and inculturation, 3, 31, 43, 84, 101; in the New Testament, 9–10; of the New World, 31–32, 47, 48, 51–52, 60, 61f, 84; by Roberto de Nobili, 5–10

F faith formation: catechesis during preaching, 60–63, 72–73, 75–77, 79–80, 85–86, 91; *catechesis familiar* (family catechesis), 74–75, 77; between first Communion and Confirmation, 65, 77; and generational differences, 91; sacramental preparation for adults, 83–84; sacramental preparation for children, 74–77, 83–84; teaching parents how to teach their children, xiii, 72, 74–75, 77

family: *catechesis familiar* (family catechesis), 74–75, 77; central for Latino identity, 27, 59–60, 83, 104; confession of family sins, 27, 76, 86, 87; difficulties in Latino families, 34; Holy Family, 98; sacramentality of, 59–60, 65, 83, 103
Fernandez, Eduardo, 25nn6–7, 37n2, 41n9, 41n11, 47n1, 48nn1–5, 57, 74nn4–6
Fernandez, Goncalo, 6–7, 9
first Communion, 75–76, 83
first Reconciliation, 74, 76–77, 83
Francis, Pope, vii–viii, ix, xii, 67, 103, 117, 119
funerals, 21, 89–91

G Gante de, Pedro, 60
Garcia, Sixto, 42
Garrido, Ann, 3
godparents, 65, 67, 70, 72–73, 75, 77, 79, 80, 84, 85, 87, 103
Goizueta, Roberto, 25–27, 41, 43, 44–45, 50–54, 57–59, 73, 83n1
Gomez, José (Archbishop), 12, 13f
Groome, Thomas, 12
Guadalupe. *See* Our Lady of Guadalupe
Gutierrez, Gustavo, 65

H high-context/low-content, 64–65
Hinduism, 6–8

Hispanic Catholicism:
  demographic statistics, viii–ix, 11, 101; family-centered identity, 27, 59–60, 83, 104; generational differences, 2, 78–79; vitality of, 11–18; worldview of U.S. Latinos, 29–35. *See also* Hispanic popular religion; sacramentality
Hispanic moment: as gift to the U.S. Catholic Church, 24, 37, 101; practical ways to respond to, 101–5; preparing priests and seminarians for, xii, 14, 18, 21–22, 28; and theology of communion, 21–28, 104–5
Hispanic popular religion: contrasted with Anglo-Catholicism, 41, 52; historical roots in Latin America, 41–43, 101; historical roots in Spanish Catholicism, 47–54, 84, 102; home as locus for, 41–42, 101; and inculturation of the Gospel, 3, 31, 43, 84, 101; and liturgical year, 93–99; noninstitutional nature of, 41–42, 52–54, 101, 102–3; relationship to official Tradition, 42–45, 102. *See also* Our Lady of Guadalupe; sacramentality
Holy Family, 98
Hoover, Brett, 69–70

I icon, 61–63
immigrants: assimilation of, 22–23; demographic trends in the U.S., 1–2, 14–15; nineteenth-century European immigrants, xi, 2, 11, 22–23, 41; undocumented immigrants, 15–16, 34; and worldview of U.S. Latinos, 33–34
inculturation, 3, 31, 43, 84, 101
India, 5–10
individualism, 27–28
insider-outsider perspective, 69–70

J Jesuits, 5–10
Jesus Christ: as major symbol for Hispanic popular religion, 30, 58, 59, 103; modeling cross-cultural preaching, 9–10, 23; in Rublev's Trinity icon, 61–63; and the Samaritan woman, 15–16, 23, 66
John Paul II, Pope, 40, 45
Johnson, Luke Timothy, 3
Juan Diego, Saint, 31–32, 48, 58, 59, 110–11, 113–14

L *lazo* (wedding cord), 84–85
liturgical year, 93–99
Los Angeles Religious Education Congress, 17
Luke, Saint, 96

M *mañanitas*, 14, 32, 40, 98
marriage, 25, 83–86
Mary, Mother of God: Hispanic feast days, 94–98; as model for Hispanic women, 80, 85. *See also* Our Lady of Guadalupe
Matovina, Timothy, 12, 22–23
mestizaje (mixture), 43, 51–52, 101

metanoia (conversion), 28
Mexico/Mexican culture: deep faith and piety, 13–14; indigenous peoples of, 31–32, 39f, 41, 43, 47, 48, 52, 59, 84, 101; Puebla region, 94, 96, 98; significance of Our Lady of Guadalupe, 13, 31–32, 33, 37–38, 52; Spanish conquest of, 31, 47, 48, 49; traditional saints' celebrations, 94–97
Michael, Saint, 94–95
Moehler, Johann Adam, 25

N Nicolas Tolentino, Saint, 94, 95f, 96
Nobili, Roberto de, 5–10

O oils, 77, 88
O'Meara, Thomas, 51
Ospino, Hosffman, vii–ix, 1, 12
Our Lady of Guadalupe: apparition to Juan Diego, 31–32, 48, 59, 110–11, 113–14; and Hispanic sacramentality, 30–35, 40, 58–59; liturgical celebrations and cultural traditions, 14, 32–33, 40, 98, 111–12, 114–15; role in wedding liturgy, 85; significance for Mexican Catholicism, 13, 31–32, 33, 37–38, 52, 60

P *padrinos* (godparents). *See* godparents
parents: bring their children for sacraments, 70–80, 83; and difficulties in Latino families, 34; preaching to, 70–73, 78–79; teaching parents to pass on the faith to their children, xi, xiii, 72, 74–75, 77
pastoral ministry to the sick and dying, 21–22, 88–91
Paul, Saint, 9–10, 23
Pecklers, Keith, 44
performance, 67–68, 115n13
popular religion. *See* Hispanic popular religion
Posadas, 42f, 98
preaching: to bilingual congregations, 78–79; challenges of cross-cultural preaching, 2–4; to children and youth, 75–80; conversational style, 63–64, 65–66, 78, 116n16; examples of cross-cultural preaching, 5–10, 23; feedback on, 104; and importance of relationships, 64–66; to intergenerational congregations, 2, 78–79; lifelong learning and humility, 107; oral aspects of, 63–66, 78, 103, 116n16; to parents and godparents, 70–73, 78–79; as performance, 67–68, 115n13; preparation for, viii, 104; at sacramental celebrations, 70–80, 85–86; use of testimony, 66–67, 78, 103–4; visual elements of, 60–63, 78, 103. *See also* sample sermons
presentación (presentation of children), 73–74
Pro, Blessed Miguel, 97
Protestantism, 33, 37–38, 80–81

Protestant Reformation, 48–49, 52, 53

Q *quinceañera*, 73, 79–80

R Reconciliation. *See* confession
Reconquista (reconquest), 47, 48, 52
rosary, 21, 41, 75, 84, 85, 91, 95–96, 102

S sacramentality: expressed in preaching, 60–68, 78, 103–4, 115n13, 116n16; of the family, 59–60, 65, 83, 103; historical roots in Spanish Catholicism, 48–54; major symbols of Hispanic popular religion, 30–35, 37, 57–59, 103
sacraments. *See* anointing of the sick; Baptism; confession; Confirmation; Eucharist; marriage
saints: archangels, 94–95; Juan Diego, 31–32, 48, 58, 59, 110–11, 113–14; Luke, 96; Michael, 94–95; Miguel Pro, 97; Nicolas Tolentino, 94, 95f, 96; Paul, 9–10, 23; Pope John Paul II, 40, 45
Samaritan woman, 15–16, 23, 66
sample sermons: for 3rd Sunday in Advent (Year A), 109–15; for 24th Sunday in Ordinary Time (Year B), 115–19; on social justice, 15–16
seminary formation, xii, 14, 18, 21–22
sensus fidelium, 43, 44

shared parishes, viii, 2, 16
Smith, Christian, xi, xiii
social justice, 15–16
Spain, 47–54, 84, 101

T Testera, Jacobo de, 60
testimony, 66–67, 78, 103–4
Tradition, 42–45, 102
Trent, Council of, 48–49, 102
Trinity, 25–27, 61–63

U Vatican I, Council of, 53
V Encuentro, 12, 17–18, 81
vocation, 115–19

W weddings, 84–85
women: grandmothers as faith leaders, 42, 101; hearing confessions of, 86, 87–88; responsibility for handing on faith and culture, 32, 87
worldviews, 29–35
Wright, N. T., 29–30

Y young adults, 80–81

Z Zumarraga, Juan de (Archbishop), 31, 48, 59, 110–11, 113–14

Also Available
from
The Catholic University of America Press

A Primer of Pastoral Spanish
by Michael J. McGrath

Pope Francis and The Search for God in América:
The Significance of His Early Visits to the Americas
edited by Maria Clara Bingemer and Peter J. Casarella

Black Catholic Studies Reader: History and Theology
edited by David J. Endres

Native American Catholic Studies Reader: History and Theology
edited by David J. Endres

The Eucharistic Vision of Laudato Si':
Praise, Conversion, and Integral Ecology
by Lucas Briola

The Power of Patristic Preaching: The Word in Our Flesh
by Andrew Hofer, OP; Foreword by Paul M. Blowers

The Art of Preaching: A Theological and Practical Primer
by Daniel Cardo

A Guide to Formation Advising for Seminarians
by Edward McCormack

Understanding the Diaconate:
Historical, Theological, and Sociological Foundations
by W. Shawn McKnight

Mysteries of the Lord's Prayer: Wisdom from the Early Church
by John Gavin

A Spiritual Theology of the Priesthood:
The Mystery of Christ and the Mission of the Priest
by Dermot Power

Amen: Jews, Christians, and Muslims Keep Faith with God
by Patrick Ryan

Introduction to Sacramental Theology:
Signs of Christ in the Flesh
by José Granados

Bread from Heaven: An Introduction to the Theology of the Eucharist
by Bernhard Blankenhorn

Seeing with the Eyes of the Heart:
Cultivating a Sacramental Imagination in an Age of Pornography
edited by Elizabeth T. Groppe

The Apostle Paul and His Letters: An Introduction
by James B. Prothro

Jesus Becoming Jesus: A Theological Interpretation of the Synoptic Gospels
by Thomas G. Weinandy

Piercing the Clouds: Lectio Divina *and Preparation for Ministry*
edited by Kevin Zilverberg and Scott Carl

Be Opened! The Catholic Church and Deaf Culture
by Marlana Portolano

Biomedicine and Beatitude:
An Introduction to Catholic Bioethics (Second Edition)
by Nicanor Pier Giorgio Austriaco

Renewing Catholic Schools: How to Regain a Catholic Vision in a Secular Age
edited by R. Jared Staudt

The Priesthood, Mystery of Faith: Priestly Ministry in the Magisterium of John Paul II
by Nilson Leal de Sá

Origins of Catholic Words: A Discursive Dictionary
by Anthony Lo Bello

Many Tongues, One Faith: A History of Franciscan Parish Life in the United States
by David J. Endres

Justice and Mercy Have Met:
Pope Francis and the Reform of the Marriage Nullity Process
edited by Kurt Martens

A Service of Love: Papal Primacy, the Eucharist, and Church Unity
by Paul McPartlan

Catholic Witness in Health Care: Practicing Medicine in Truth and Love
edited by John M. Travaline and Louise A. Mitchell

The Dry Wood: Catholic Women Writers
by Caryll Houselander